RELIGION AND SCIENCE:

DECONSTRUCTING A MODERN PARADIGM

A Critique of Religion as a Socially
Constructed Device of Modernity

Rodney W. Tussing

Public Philosophy Press
Phoenix, Arizona 2019
First Edition published in 2019 by Public Philosophy Press, LLC

Library of Congress Cataloging-in-Publication Data pending

Religion and Science: Deconstructing a Modern Paradigm

Includes bibliographic references
Includes index
ISBN: 9781732801806

1. Title. 2. Religion 3. Philosophy of Religion 4. Philosophy 5. Science

Cover design by Beth Ellen Nagle

Printed in the United States of America
This book is printed on acid-free paper

www.publicphilosophypress.com

Table of Contents

Preface

I, LIKE MANY others in the West, went through the public education system where I learned about the wonders of science and how the employment of the scientific method has produced the miracles of technology that so define our modern civilization. Through this method of systematically counting, weighing, and measuring data, which has characterized natural science since the 17th century, the world has been blessed with the benefits of subduing and taking dominion over it. The fruits of these efforts have produced technologies that have often been described as ingenious, with the effect of awe and wonder, and indeed, considered "miraculous."

The achievements of science, and its method for acquiring knowledge about the world, have often been placed in contrast to the traditionally received authority and truth claims of the Christian Church, and particularly its most noted miracle of the resurrection of Christ. The difference between them, of course, is that the "miracles of science" can be empirically verified and duplicated and the biblical miracles cannot. This contrast, which is often depicted as a tension between science and religion, has extended beyond just miracles, and touches only the surface of the much deeper epistemological issue of knowledge v. opinion. Is science based on knowledge and religion based only on opinion?

As a young student, I began to see that these deliverables of science were only one aspect of an apparent larger dichotomy between science and what I understood to be religion. Science seemed to be offering a view of the world that was in conflict with a so-called religious view of the world. It led me to then consider the paramount questions regarding truth and error, knowledge and opinion, faith and reason. Were these views on religion and science actually at odds with each other—was one true and the other false—or was something else going on? How were these ostensible tensions to be understood and resolved?

In this short book I consider the relationship between what is called religion and what is called science. I argue that the fundamental issue that divides the two views is an epistemological one. That is, judgements and beliefs about the nature of reality at the most basic level are presupposed by both religion and science and are not only different, but in fact contradictory. It then logically follows that two belief systems with contradictory beliefs about the ultimate nature of the universe are going to be at odds with each other. The meaning of each of these terms, religion and science, will be developed in order to make this point clear. Can one view be rationally justified and, therefore, claim knowledge? This epistemological question and issue will be explored and, hopefully, convincingly answered.

This book, then, essentially unpacks, critiques, and deconstructs the divide between these two categories of religion and science. It exposes the misleading way that the relationship has been taught, understood, and received by successive generations; which I call a "modern paradigm."

Acknowledgments

MANY HAVE CONTRIBUTED to the development and publication of this book and to whom I am greatly indebted. Thank you to David and Kelly Burton, Owen Anderson, Mevin Joshi, Robert Burns, Linell Cady, and Joel Gereboff who read portions of the manuscript and offered helpful feedback. David and Kelly also provided help in the publication process for which I am grateful. A special thank you goes to Surrendra Gangadean whose mentoring over the years and especially for his insight into issues such as the one addressed in this book, provided the necessary inspiration to engage in this particular topic. And finally, this work would never have been completed without the self-less love and support of my wonderful wife, Jamie, to whom I am most indebted.

1

Introduction

OVER THE LAST one hundred years or so, religious studies have flourished in the educational institutions of the West. The idea of religion, once the exclusive domain of Christian thinkers and believers, has now expanded to include a multitude of diverse belief systems and practices. Much of the dialogue in the academy today continues to focus on questions relating to theories of religion such as; what is it? why is it? can it be defined? and how does it relate to science? These, and similar types of questions, will be the focus of this work.

While considering these questions and their importance, I will, however, approach the topic from a different perspective. Due to the tension that has developed between the idea of religion and non-religion, particularly in light of science and claims to exclusive knowledge, a different and more clear approach is now necessary. I will explore the idea of religion v. non-religion and highlight some of the difficulties associated with this 'paradigm,' and offer an alternative scheme that provides a more plausible way to divide the world's belief systems. And as a bi-product of the discussion, I will also question and challenge the validity of the term, religion, as it is popularly used today. Put simply, this work will argue that the popular religion/science paradigm produced by modernity is not valid and needs to be deconstructed.

That there is such a thing as 'religion' in the world few would deny. Everyone today, at least in the West, seems to know what religion is and what it is not. A familiar account is that religion can be best explained as a certain set of beliefs, rules, and practices for living. It is typically thought to be belief in a transcendent reality, one that is not part of this material world, one that is holy, or sacred, and makes certain things in this world holy or sacred. The idea of religion consists of performing particular rituals at particular times and it is often thought to be a belief in a higher power, a God or gods. Additionally, it is thought to be a set of beliefs that explain and interpret life and, by implication, the nature of ultimate reality. To believe in this type of transcendent reality and to perform the corresponding prescribed behaviors or rituals is to be religious, so the typical account goes.

We in the West use the term, religion, freely and assume that everyone knows what we are talking about. We refer to Christianity, Judaism, Islam, and Buddhism, for example, as religions and the adherents of these as those who are religious. There are the faithful, those who follow their religion more or less consciously and consistently, there are those who are somewhat religious, and, of course, there are those who have no religion at all. The common understanding seems to be that there is religion and non-religion, religious people and non-religious people, and there are religious views and non-religious views.

At what can be called the 'popular' level, the term religion, as just summarized, appears to be clearly understood and can be differentiated using the descriptions listed above from what it is not, thus producing two separate categories—religion and non-religion. Even without an explicit scholarly definition of religion these two categories are evident in virtually every area of life. For instance, an average bookstore will have numerous book sections including one on religion. Historians speak of religious histories and news analysts report on the latest happenings in the religious world.

This is such a common distinction that many identify themselves with one category or the other and often may feel antagonism from the alternative view. Critics, such as the group known as 'the new atheists,' express their disdain for religion and assert the need to abolish it favoring the idea of a world without religion—a totally secular world.[1] Examples depicting religion as a distinct category are endless, thus establishing a type of 'belief paradigm'—religion and non-religion—a particular way of looking at the world that has become a commonly accepted conceptual scheme. These two categories have been received by the modern Western mindset and often without much critical thought. It is considered a given.

After many years of teaching Philosophy, Philosophy of Religion, and World Religions at the college level, I have become convinced that the dichotomy between a religious perspective, or worldview,[2] and a non-reli-

---

1   Philosopher of religion, Alvin Plantinga, identifies the "new atheists" as Richard Dawkins, Daniel Dennett, Christopher Hitchens, and Sam Harris with an aim to "run roughshod over religion." "[T]hey attribute most of the ills of the world to religion....religious belief is unreasonable and irrational," *Where the Conflict Really Lies* (Oxford: Oxford University Press, 2011) x-xi. Victor Stenger would also include himself in this group and has addressed the relationship between contemporary atheism and religion in his work, *The New Atheism: Taking a Stand for Science and Reason* (New York: Prometheus Books, 2009). The naturalistic claims of the "new atheists" will be developed more in what follows.

2   The term 'worldview' as used in this project means a unified comprehensive system—a metanarrative—that attempts to present a coherent view of existence by explaining the meaning and purpose of the world and life in its totality. As human beings, we tend to subscribe to and place ourselves into a grand, or master, narrative. Christianity, as an example, is one of many. George Lindbeck and William Abraham come very close to the intended meaning. Lindbeck writes, "[R]eligions are seen as comprehensive interpretive schemes, usually embodied in myths or narratives and heavily ritualized, which structure human experience and understanding of self and world....a religion can be viewed as a kind of cultural and/or linguistic framework or medium that shapes the entirety of life and thought." *The Nature of Doctrine* (Philadelphia: The Westminster Press, 1984) 32-3. Abraham writes, "Religious belief should be assessed as a rounded whole rather then taken in stark isolation. Christianity, for example, like other world faiths, is a complex, large-scale system of belief which must be seen as a whole before it is assessed. To break it up into disconnected parts is to mutilate and distort its character. We can, of course, distinguish certain elements in the Christian faith, but we must still stand back and see it as a complex interaction of these elements. We need

---

gious one is deeply-seated in the Western consciousness and continues to be the putative position, which is not surprising since no strong challenge to it appears to be forthcoming.[3] The religious and non-religious categories are often characterized and exemplified by the religion and science model. Many students enter the classroom presupposing the generally accepted divide between religion and science as popularly understood and perceive a tension between them. They tend to insist that a 'scientific view,' prima facie, is a valid and justifiable alternative to a religious view.

In keeping with the popular understanding, students consistently present the scientific view as the non-religious view—the neutral, publicly held view. Religion, thought by many scholars to be notoriously difficult to define, is believed to be a particular bias based on faith or belief, personal feelings, or family tradition, and is not grounded in knowledge and facts. Put simply, a religious view lacks verifiable evidence and proof, it is often said, but nonetheless is considered a tenable view by many.

Science, on the other hand, is about the pursuit of neutral brute facts obtained through the use of reason and the scientific method resulting in knowledge that can be publicly verified. The scientific view is commonly expressed as a naturalistic view, a materialistic conception of the universe—one in which only the physical, material world can be known with certainty. A non-material, or spiritual, realm is considered non-verifiable and, therefore, not based on science. Whether the spirit realm exists or not

---

to see it as a metaphysical system, as a world view, that is total in its scope and range." *An Introduction to the Philosophy of Religion* (Englewood Cliffs, NJ: Prentice Hall, 1985) 104. For a detailed exploration of the concept see David Naugle's, *Worldview: The History of a Concept* (Grand Rapids: W.B. Eerdmans Publishing Co., 2002). The worldview idea will be dealt with more in the final chapter of this work.

3   As a work of interest here see Talal Asad's, *Genealogies of Religion* (Baltimore: The Johns Hopkins University Press, 1993). In it he explores the idea of religion as a construct of European modernity from the perspective of anthropology and questions the adequacy of Western modernity as a universal ideological model. Three additional works arguing a similar theme are Daniel Dubuisson's, *The Western Construction of Religion* (Baltimore: Johns Hopkins University Press, 1993) Russell McCutcheon's, *Manufacturing Religion* (New York: Oxford University Press, 1997), and Timothy Fitzgerald's, *The Ideology of Religious Studies* (New York: Oxford University Press, 2000).

is not knowable. Those, then, who would affirm a religious view would be doing so based upon their personal opinion, or a blind faith, and not on proof or evidence. Only beliefs that can be empirically verified qualify for dialogue in the public square with all other beliefs to be considered private.

In support of the scientific view, students will often make an immediate appeal to the voices of the leading lights of science, such as physicist Stephen Hawking's authoritative statement, "[i]t is not necessary to invoke God to light the blue touch paper and set the universe going," or to biologist Richard Dawkins' general thesis, "the factual premise of religion—the God hypothesis—is untenable."[4]

While many students tend to be accepting of alternative views to science, some are less tolerant and have other favorite authoritative figures like Sam Harris and Victor Stenger to whom they appeal. Science writer, Sam Harris, is a contributor to the perceived tension and intolerance between science and religion and sees a clash between them. He emphasizes his disdain for religion when he says, "[w]hich of our present practices will appear most ridiculous from the point of view of those future generations that might yet survive the folly of the present? It is hard to imagine that our religious preoccupations will not top the list."[5] Physicist, Victor Stenger, when speaking of religion, makes a similar comment;

Faith is absurd and dangerous and we look forward to the day, no matter how distant, when the human race finally abandons it. Reason is a noble substitute, proven by its success. Religion is an intellectual and moral sickness that cannot endure forever if we believe at all in human progress.[6]

---

4 Stephen Hawking and Leonard Mlodinow, *The Grand Design* (New York: Bantam Books, 2010) 180, and Richard Dawkins, *The God Delusion* (New York: Houghton Mifflin Co. 2006) 189.

5 Sam Harris, *The End of Faith* (New York: W.W. Norton & Co., 2005) 48.

6 Victor Stenger, *The New Atheists: Taking a Stand for Science and Reason* (New York: Prometheus Books, 2009) 244.

Such forceful and authoritative rancor needs explanation. Why the strong divide? The exclusively Western perceived distinction between religion and non-religion, as just illustrated, is oftentimes portrayed as facts v. opinion, or more moderately expressed as knowledge (science) v. faith (religion).

Western modernity has produced two categories of belief with these two entities, science and religion, as a common way to express them.[7] But, why these two? A distinction has been made, but what are the essential differences between them that justifies the categories? Are there valid reasons for these categories and for the responses elicited by the scholars just mentioned, or are they what philosopher of science, Thomas Kuhn, calls a product of 'normal science,' a 'paradigm?' That is, as Kuhn explains, "achievements that some particular scientific community acknowledges for a time as supplying the foundation for its further practice."[8] The implication here is that the idea of normalcy is only temporary—for a particular time and context. While commitment to the same paradigm provides the basis for a consensus on particular research traditions, it is "sufficiently open-ended to leave all sorts of problems for the redefined group of practitioners to resolve."[9]

In a similar way, a paradigm has developed in modern history for how to understand the relationship between religion and science. The divide has become commonly accepted, but has issues that need to be more carefully examined and defined. Some of those problems are now coming to light and in need of closer critical assessment and resolution. This paradigm of modernity is flawed and needs to be deconstructed.

---

7   Chapter two will define Modernity in more detail. For now it is to be understood as the time following the European Renaissance, Protestant Reformation, and the work of Descartes and Locke that was characterized by individualism and subjectivism and a move away from authoritarian standards and toward objective standards that are determined in isolation from the values and practices of particular cultures.

8   Thomas Kuhn, *The Structure of Scientific Revolutions* (Chicago: University of Chicago Press, 1962) 10.

9   Kuhn, *The Structure,* 10.

1.1 A Modern Tension and Presuppositions

This project will identify and respond to some of the tensions inherent in the current science/religion 'paradigm' by offering a detailed explanation regarding the origin and purpose of these two categories of belief as well as their differences. How are the two categories to be understood? Clearly, there is a history that has informed and produced these two ideas that have been, and continue to be, examined by anthropologists, sociologists, and historians for cultural significance. Models for how to understand the historically developed relationship between science and religion have been devised and many books have been written to explain it. These models attempt to explain the relationship of science and religion in terms of spheres of knowledge and how these spheres relate to each other, if at all.

But this project is intended to be more than an historical assessment. The validity of the paradigm itself will be critically examined and challenged. Differences between the ideas of science and religion at the most basic level will be considered. It will seek to implement the insight of philosopher, Surrendra Gangadean, with his axiom, "[c]ritical thinking is by nature presuppositional; without the more basic in place, what comes after cannot be understood."[10] What is meant by this is that all humans think and have beliefs about various things. These beliefs are held together by reason and form a 'belief system' when focusing on a particular topic.[11] Some of the beliefs within the system are more basic than others. That is, what are considered less basic beliefs are dependent upon and are

10   Surrendra Gangadean, *Philosophical Foundation: A Critical Analysis of Basic Beliefs* (Lanham: University Press of America, Inc., 2008) quoted from the preface.

11   The idea of a 'belief system' here is intended to mean logically connected beliefs, a coherence of ideas, an affirmation that a proposition, or propositions about the existence, experience, meaning, and nature of the world are true (held individually or collectively), and are more or less consciously and consistently held. The idea of a belief system is essentially a 'worldview.' Sam Harris rightly recognizes the significance of beliefs when he says, "A Belief is a lever that, once pulled, moves almost everything else in a person's life. Are you a scientist? A liberal? A racist? These are merely species of belief in action. Your beliefs define your vision of the world; they dictate your behavior; they determine your emotional responses to other human beings." *End of Faith*, 12. More on this will be discussed in the next chapter.

constructed upon more basic beliefs. Less basic beliefs are understood and have their meaning in light of more basic beliefs.

These most basic beliefs are considered foundational and are either explicitly or implicitly held. For instance, beliefs about what so-called religion is and does presuppose a more basic belief about the nature of reality. In other words, the idea of religion and how religion is expressed is embedded in one's larger view of the nature and purpose of the world and how it works.

The idea of religion is often thought to be about life's ultimate concerns and is understood in light of one's most basic belief about what ultimately exists.[12] It addresses and provides answers to fundamental questions about the nature of existence. That belief then, about what is ultimate, informs one regarding choices that are considered good, or even *the greatest good*, that are helpful for humans to understand and achieve the purpose and goal of life.

The idea of religion and the concerns associated with it can be expressed in the three traditional categories of philosophy. It is about beliefs concerning 'what is' (metaphysics), how that is known (epistemology), and how these beliefs are practiced in order to achieve 'the good' for human beings (ethics). The belief held in the area of metaphysics (what ultimately exists) serves as a foundational belief and is oftentimes not understood explicitly but is presupposed to be true. There is a systematic order to presuppositional critical thinking, from the more basic to the less basic. All human beings have beliefs and are held more or less consciously

---

12 Ivan Strenski, in his, *Thinking About Religion: An Historical Introduction to Theories of Religion,* addresses this point in his first chapter section on 'Natural Religion.' In it he states, "Those that adhered to the idea of Natural Religion typically felt that human beings therefore can *know* about ultimate truth by their own human abilities. Divine intervention is not required for people to know God, for example." (10). Here he seems to indicate that intellectual inquiry on basic issues has, historically, been equated to the idea of religion. This, of course, assumes a particular definition of the term 'religion.' (Oxford: Blackwell Publishing, 2006). See also Roy Clouser's, *The Myth of Religious Neutrality* (Notre Dame, In., University of Notre Dame Press, 2005). In this work Clouser argues that religious belief is belief in anything with eternal attributes, that is "divine per se."

and consistently.[13] This is the case whether the beliefs are of a so-called religious nature or of a practical nature.

Western discourse on religion is regularly compared and contrasted to what has come to be known as the secular. Discussion about the idea of religion and its relationship to the secular, secularism, and secularization is unavoidable, but will not be the primary focus here. It will be important in so far as theories of secularization are interrelated with Western modernity. However, the specific details of that discussion are for other projects, such as philosopher, Charles Taylor's comprehensive tome, *A Secular Age*. In his work, Taylor understands secularization to be a feature of modernity, but challenges some of the popular theories of secularization/religion and proposes an alternative explanation. He asks and attempts to answer the simple, yet complex, question undergirding the very idea of secularization; "why was it virtually impossible not to believe in God in, say, 1500 in our Western society, while in 2000 many of us find this not only easy, but even inescapable?"[14] But, as he also asks, how and why did things change? "How did the alternatives become thinkable?"[15] In other words, how did Western culture get from a position of uniformity of belief to a state of accepting alternative views? Taylor attempts to answer this. To borrow a pertinent line from Taylor, and one that fits this project, "[t]he story of what happened in the secularization of Western Christendom is so broad, and so multi-faceted, that one could write several books this length and still not do justice to it."[16]

The present project will also address Taylor's questions, but will consider them through the lens of philosophical categories. Of particular interest will be one of those categories, epistemology, and how epistemological changes helped define Western modernity and ultimately produce

---

13   Gangadean, *Philosophical Foundation*, 3.

14   Charles Taylor, *A Secular Age* (Cambridge: Harvard University Press, 2007) 25.

15   Taylor, *Secular*, 25.

16   Taylor, *Secular*, 29.

the idea of religion. I will attempt to show how changes in what qualified as knowledge produced the dichotomy in question and the resultant religion/science paradigm.

1.2 The Tension and Knowledge Claims

While the relationship between modernity, secularism, science, and religion is historically and culturally as Taylor says, multi-faceted, it will be important to keep in mind that this work will focus primarily on the epistemic component that produced the two belief categories—religion and science. That is, the significance of what qualifies as knowledge (and not opinion) will be explored as a major contributing factor in the development of the category distinction and the difference between them. Both categories claim 'to know,' however, that claim needs to be explored more fully and the meaning clarified.

To start, it seems clear from the above comments that, according to the popular understanding, one view is perceived to be based on reason and the others not. Science is based on reason and religion is not, it is often argued. This view of science has produced a perspective on the world that has come to be technically called, philosophical or metaphysical naturalism, a product of Western modernity with roots in classical Greek philosophy.[17] It is important to note here that metaphysical naturalism

---

17   For the purposes of this work, naturalism, and more specifically philosophical or metaphysical naturalism, will be considered a 'worldview' similar to the definition in footnote 2 above. Chapter two of this work will explain how it came to be considered a worldview. The basic metaphysical beliefs of this view are something similar to William Drees' statement that "naturalism assumes that all objects around us, including ourselves, consist of the stuff described by chemists in the periodic table of the elements" and that theism is irrelevant. Drees also quotes an applicable comment by Charley Hardwick that further defines naturalism, "(1) that only the world of nature is real; (2) that nature is necessary in the sense of requiring no sufficient reason beyond itself to account for its origin or ontological ground; (3) that nature as a whole may be understood without appeal to any kind of intelligence or purposive agent; and (4) that all causes are natural causes so that every natural event is itself a product of other natural events." "Religious Naturalism and Science," in Clayton and Simpson, eds. *The Oxford Handbook of Religion and Science* (New York: Oxford University Press: 2006) 110. The term 'naturalism' is not intended to mean the same as it is used by J. Samuel Preus

is distinct from methodological naturalism. Methodological naturalism is the particular approach and set of assumptions used for gathering and understanding scientific data and presupposes metaphysical naturalism. Metaphysical naturalism functions as the more basic belief, or philosophy of existence, that affirms that only a material world exists and then employs methods that interpret all the data of science according to that basic belief.

Acquiring the privileged status.

Due to the wide acceptance of this view, particularly in the Western academy, the notion that naturalism qualifies as the predominant, or privileged (favorably accepted as true and, therefore, authoritative), view of reality is pervasive.[18] It is the basis for the favored method of inquiry by many religion theorists.[19] As the authoritative view, scholars presuppose it to study the alternative 'religious' views and do research in the 'science of religion' or the 'phenomenology of religion.' It is the function of reason and science to produce the proper understanding of alternative views that purportedly reject the authority of reason and the naturalistic view, and favor fideistic dogma and tradition. Thus, even though there may be uncertainty regarding how to define religion specifically, there appears to be

---

in his, *Explaining Religion: Criticism and Theory from Bodin to Freud* (Atlanta: Scholars Press, 1996) or in Russell McCutcheon's, *Manufacturing Religion* (New York: Oxford University Press, 1997). Both of these scholars view naturalism strictly as a method "to study religion as a part of human culture and history...without the benefit of clergy." *Manufacturing Religion,* ix.

The idea of modernity in this project will be delimited and understood primarily from an epistemological perspective. As such, the focus will be on the impact of changes between pre-modern, modern, and postmodern with respect to what qualifies as knowledge. A more specific explanation will be explained in chapter two.

18   See George Marsden's, *The Soul of the American University* (New York: Oxford University Press, 1994). In this work Marsden argues that today in the American University secular naturalism is generally perceived as the only valid academic perspective and precludes alternative perspectives.

19   Including not only the classical religion theorists such as Hume, Durkheim, and Freud, but also contemporary theorists such as Pascal Boyer and Daniel Dennett.

a general consensus on what religion is and is not, which hinges on the use of reason and indicates the strength of the paradigm. This proposition will soon be borne out.

But how does one particular view attain a privileged status? There should be no doubt that the view grounded in reason and knowledge ought to be the preferred view and, as such, demands a type of privilege. There is no higher authority than reason itself. For rational human beings, to use reason consistently produces integrity and results in being human in the fullest sense. Reason and consistency also produce meaning. To use Gangadean's words, "[p]ersons as rational beings need meaning. Integrity, as a basic form of honesty, is a concern for consistency."[20] When used properly, reason also produces knowledge, which then results in particular practices. Conversely, not to use reason consistently, or to hold beliefs without proof or evidence, would be to be devoid of knowledge and integrity. Privilege, then, simply means that the view established as the most rational has a perceived preeminence.

To recognize this relationship, and in keeping with the principles of modernity, is to recognize that knowledge, or the lack of it, has an ethical component as well. The ethical feature is evident in the famous quote by English philosopher, W.K. Clifford (1845-1879), a significant figure of enlightened modernity, "it is wrong always, everywhere, and for anyone, to believe anything upon insufficient evidence."[21] He refers to this as 'the ethics of belief.' One's beliefs must be grounded in sound reasons and arguments, they must be rationally justified. Choices ought to be grounded in knowledge and not opinion. Modernity requires rational evidence as a necessary condition for belief as expressed above by naturalists, Hawking, Dawkins, and the others. The significance of these points is that there is a necessary relationship between belief, knowledge, and practice—the categories of philosophy.

---

20   Gangadean, *Philosophical Foundation*, 143-148.

21   W.K. Clifford, *The Ethics of Belief*, quoted in Steven Cahn, ed., *Ten Essential Texts in the Philosophy of Religion* (New York: Oxford University Press, 2005) 372.

Modernity and the epistemological shift.

The epistemological shift that has taken place between what has been termed modernity and the present age, the postmodern, has challenged the primacy of Reason as the ultimate adjudicator for knowledge, truth, and error. The postmodern critic asks, is all of this emphasis on reason anything more than the on-going misguided promotion of the Enlightenment dream? Some have argued that the ideals of modernity have failed and that Reason has been overstated and over extended. Postmodernity has proposed a more 'chastened' view of Reason, one that limits Reason's capability, which raises questions regarding the possibility of any privileged view. More detail on this will be discussed in chapter five.

In spite of the postmodern challenge, naturalism has held fast to Enlightenment ideals and the deliverables of Reason and has been the privileged position for most of the twentieth century and into the twenty-first. It has claimed to be the most reasonable position supported by the facts. Part of the explanation for its success has been due to the failure of theism to produce rational justification for its truth claims, thus the declaration that religion is based on a blind faith and not facts and reason. Some would say that theism, indeed, all forms of religion, is non-cognitive—not capable of producing knowledge.

To avoid this same fate, naturalism will eventually face the same critical tribunal. For it to succeed and continue as the privileged view, naturalism will have to demonstrate that it is indeed based on a rationally justified, sound argument. It must produce reasons that prove its first principles—its most basic beliefs regarding ultimate reality. That is, it must be shown to be based on more than dogma, opinion, and tradition—the claims charged against theism. What is believed to exist ultimately must be shown by naturalists to be clear to reason—readily knowable.

This notion regarding the significance of Reason raises an important question; if naturalism is based on facts and is the most rational view, then why would any rational person opt for an alternative view? The obvious response by many naturalists is that a rational person would not. Hence the charge that religion is non-cognitive and believers have no rational basis for their belief seems to substantiate the need for a category distinction.

1.3 Explaining the Tension and Dichotomy

Given the very real conflict here, how, then, is this issue to be explained? What is apparent is that in the commonly accepted paradigm there are two distinct categories of belief systems. One category consists of a naturalistic view of reality and the other category consists of a multitude of alternative belief systems that are diverse, yet unified in their rejection of naturalism.

Is religion a social construct?

While the idea of naturalism is adequately clear as explained above, of what, then, does the category called religion consist? What is religion and, more specifically, what is a religious belief and a religious belief system? Is religion a thing in itself, an intrinsic part of human nature (*sui generis*) that all humans innately possess? That is, do all humans have a religious inclination by nature that elicits a particular kind of belief? Is it something that is identifiable that can be researched and studied as a science and as a cultural phenomenon? Does it require a particular discipline that can justify inquiry and a 'science of religion' or 'phenomenology of religion'?[22] Is it something that can be isolated and scientifically analyzed as many scholars in the field of religious studies, past and present, have said that it is? Or is it as other scholars have argued—just an ideological, socio-political or psychological construct, a bi-product of culture, and not an isolatable thing in itself to be studied?

---

22   See Mircea Eliade's, *The Sacred and the Profane* (New York: Harcourt Brace &Co., 1959), an illustration of *sui generis* religion and Russell McCutcheon's *Manufacturing Religion* in which the idea is critically assessed.

Some contemporary scholars have attempted to answer these questions by exposing the idea of religion as a modern Western invention, an ideology, a social construct that has been created, whether consciously or unconsciously, for the purpose of legitimating authority and power within institutions.[23] Jonathan Z. Smith is one of those scholars who contends that the idea of religion is a general category of diverse views about the nature of existence and the world that has been socially constructed. Smith argues that "[t]here is no data for religion. Religion is solely the creation of the scholar's study. It is created for the scholar's analytic purposes by his imaginative acts of comparison and generalization. Religion has no independent existence apart from the academy."[24] This idea will be examined in more detail in the next chapter.

Yet another account of so-called religion may be just as bold as J. Z. Smith's. Perhaps defining religion is self-evident. A common denominator of all that is called religion is that they are all contrary to, in some form or another, the major tenets of naturalism. As such, these 'religious belief systems' form a part of a socially constructed category that can be defined by what it is not. Therefore, a separate category is required for all belief systems that fundamentally oppose naturalism. Additionally, it can be convincingly argued that these diverse alternative belief systems have all been constructed for the purpose of providing an interpretation and an explanation of particular people's life experiences.

But understood in this way, another important question is raised. Could it not also be the case that naturalism, like religion, has been socially constructed for the purpose of interpreting and explaining the data of experience? There is one category that affirms metaphysical naturalism to be true and another category consisting of all other belief systems that rejects metaphysical naturalism. The idea of religion, as a separate catego-

---

23 For more on this idea see Timothy Fitzgerald's, *The Ideology of Religious Studies* (New York: Oxford University Press, 2000) and Russell McCutcheon's, *Manufacturing Religion*.

24 Jonathan Z. Smith, *Imagining Religion: From Babylon to Jonestown* (Chicago: University of Chicago Press, 1982) xi.

ry, can now be seen as a totalizing concept developed by modernity that allows for grouping disparate, non-naturalism affirming beliefs or belief systems. This establishes the two-category idea, but more discussion and clarification on this is needed. A 'definition' and additional qualification for the term 'religion' is important for this project and will also be addressed in greater detail in the next chapter.

1.4 Thesis Explained

It will be argued in this work that the religion category and the two-category approach to the world's belief systems, commonly understood as religion and science, is inadequate and ought to be deconstructed and reformulated. It is time for a 'paradigm shift' in the Kuhnian sense, that is to say, a change in the way the idea of religion is conceived that will, of necessity, realign the relationship between so-called religion and science. Both the idea of religion and naturalism can be considered ideologies, belief frameworks, or worldviews that are grounded on presupposed basic beliefs. Moreover, how can there be profitable discourse when one of the major terms used in the discussion is determined undefinable?

Objectives considered.

These points will be addressed in what follows with three separate objectives in mind. The first objective will assess the origin of the category dichotomy and the historical thought that produced it. The second will be a more critical analysis, exposing the major epistemic issues regarding the way the categories of religion and science have been established with the ultimate goal being to deconstruct the existing dichotomy and paradigm. And thirdly, after the existing paradigm is deconstructed, a proposal that more accurately divides the world's belief systems will be offered along with a methodology for more fruitful inquiry.

Once the artificial paradigm is removed a more objective assessment of the world's belief systems can be made. These three objectives will combine to illustrate not only that the present divide between science and religion is illegitimate and unacceptable, but also that the belief that naturalism ought to be the privileged view is unfounded.

Although this work is not a study in anthropological or socio-political value theory, it will, however, show how the foundational beliefs addressed herein form the basis for such values and theories.[25] Rather, it is a type of 'first order' work. That is, it will address and explore the first principles, or presuppositions, upon which ideas such as religion, naturalism, secularism, and religion theory are constructed. While all of these ideas will be mentioned, the amount of emphasis on each will need to be limited to the context at hand—with a more specific reference to epistemology and the ideas of religion and naturalism.

The methodology used in the project will be at once historical and philosophical—although limited to epistemology and the ideas of religion and naturalism. To be more specific, the concept of knowledge and what qualifies as knowledge played an important role in the development of Western modernity and, therefore, in the formation of the ideas of religion and naturalism.

The project will be historical by showing the progressive maturation of the naturalistic view that ultimately produced the category of religion. It will also be philosophical by revealing the intellectual challenges to theism that permitted an exclusively naturalistic perspective on the data of science and the idea of religion to gain dominance, as well as to critically assess the inherent shortcomings of each. This combination will expose

---

25 Manuel Vasquez, in his work, *More Than Belief: A Materialist Theory of Religion* (New York: Oxford University Press, 2011) uses what he call "a non-reductive materialist framework" to describe how particular so-called religious believers appeal to the supernatural to "build their identities, narratives, practices, and environments. Thus it behooves scholars of religion to take seriously the native actor's lived world and to explore the biological, social, and historical conditions that make religious experiences possible as well as the effects these experiences have on self, culture, and nature."(3). Vasquez assumes the category distinction and illustrates, at least descriptively, how a so-called religion functions as a combination of beliefs and comprehensive cultural practices.

the inadequacy of the two categories as they are currently expressed and the need for a reformulation.

The project is essentially a work in the philosophy of the idea of religion, tracing some of the intellectual developments that have not only informed and shaped the academic and popular conceptions of the relationship between religion and science, but have also shaped university Religious Studies programs as well.

With a metaphysical and epistemological focus, it will show that the scientific worldview of modernity has, with a large measure of intention, constructed the separation between science and religion for the purpose of claiming exclusive rights to what qualifies as knowledge and deems those views in the religion category as non-cognitive. Consequently, what forms and divides the two categories at the most basic level is the claim to knowledge, and virtually all modern academic disciplines presuppose, either explicitly or implicitly, the validity of this claim. Both categories have sought, and continue to seek, rational justification for their claims to knowledge.[26] Each claims to have knowledge and since the Enlightenment era specific criteria have been established to determine if it is indeed possessed.[27] But according to strict Enlightenment standards both religion and naturalism, in spite of their claims, have fallen short.

Modernity's view of science, as expressed by philosophical naturalism, has been constructed on a foundation insufficient to produce the knowledge and authority that it claims to have. It claims to have knowledge of the nature of existence, which is essentially a statement about the nature of reality. But this claim, it will be shown, is based on unproven epistemic assumptions and, therefore, cannot be considered knowledge.

---

26 Beliefs require justification in order to be considered knowledge and to be considered true. The most basic beliefs of worldviews, the first principles, need to be justified by reason in order to avoid dogmatism and/or fideism. So-called religious belief has not been able to do this and, consequently, has not been considered knowledge. Presumably, naturalism can justify its most basic beliefs and can then claim knowledge. The following will examine that claim.

27 Chapter three will identify modernity's qualifications for knowledge.

Yet it still makes the claim to knowledge and to Reason without offering rational proof for its first principles, or presuppositions—the same charge made by naturalists against theism, which was jettisoned as a valid position for lack of proof.

Theism was marginalized and deemed irrelevant because it could not rationally justify its most basic belief regarding existence and ultimate reality—that a non-material reality exists that is infinite, eternal, and immutable, and has created the universe. When naturalism is critically examined at the most basic level it will be shown that, like the charge against theism, it also cannot justify its most basic belief in a material only universe, thus dissolving the dichotomy. If neither category can demonstrate knowledge at the most basic level, then the fundamental basis for the divide between them collapses. Consequentially, without rationally justifying one category or the other, skepticism and nihilism become the only alternative.

Project thesis statement.

Chapter six will explain the above points on justification in more detail. It will explore the possibility of a valid foundation for knowledge. Moreover, without justification for the claim to knowledge, there is no basis for privilege. Thus, the thesis of this project will become apparent, that *the category distinction between science and religion as presently conceived is a fabrication by modernity and needs to be deconstructed and reformulated.* If neither category can produce a basis for knowledge, then opinion and skepticism are the only options. Fruitful and meaningful discourse then ceases. Additionally, the term, religion, as used by modernity, has been misappropriated leaving the status of the term, and the category itself, unfounded and a source of confusion.

This work will attempt to bring clarity. It will not be an argument supporting the idea of religion nor will it promote postmodern skepticism.[28] While it challenges the privileged position of naturalism, it is not an attempt to prove the existence of God. Rather, it is a study that explores and ultimately deconstructs today's understanding of the relationship between the idea of religion and science as two separate categories of belief, the currently popular paradigm, and replaces it with an alternative conceptual scheme.

As a necessary bi-product of the discussion, the concept of privilege will also be addressed. A distinction between the perspective of religion and the perspective of science has been made historically, but the difference at the most basic level has not been made clear. The intent here is to tear down a stronghold that has not, and is not, effectively serving the academy by facilitating growth in understanding, but instead, has promoted confusion. Such an undertaking will require the critical analysis of the presuppositions of both in order to discover the essential difference between their belief frameworks. Once clearly identified, it will be evident that the dichotomy and current assignment of privilege is not rationally defendable.

The primary focus for the project will, therefore, be on the theoretical basis for the distinction and differences between the two categories, religion and science (non-religion), which have been constructed and defined by a particular hermeneutic of Western modernity. Informed by Western modernity, the meanings, purpose, and even validity of these categories, have become a part of the cultural landscape. However, failure to fully understand the significance of the issues at hand has brought confusion to the academic study of the idea of religion and of science.

Current debate asks the questions; what is it that is to be studied? Whose methodology is to be used in the academy, the naturalist's or the theist's, or neither? Considered undefinable, who then has the right per-

---

28   Postmodern thinkers have challenged the objectivity of science and epistemic realism, which ultimately leads to skepticism. While this work addresses the issue and its significance, it is not arguing for it as the sole argument against naturalism. See Michael Ruse, *Mysteries of Mysteries: Is Evolution a Social Construction?* (Cambridge: Harvard University Press, 1999) and Keith Parsons, ed., *The Science Wars* (New York: Prometheus Books, 2003).

spective on the idea of religion? Or, more importantly, what does the term, religion, signify?

These are philosophical questions and issues that need philosophical answers. As a work in the philosophy of religion, it will critically analyze the epistemic presuppositions upon which the idea of religion has been constructed. And, since religion has become integrally related to science and in some sense, by modern assessments, subordinate to it in its contention for truth and knowledge, it necessarily addresses the epistemic presuppositions of philosophical naturalism, modernity's interpretation of the data of science. It will trace some of the intellectual developments prompted by the religion/science relationship that have, more or less, consciously informed and shaped all academic fields of inquiry. The primary focus will be at the foundational level, including the field of Religious Studies within the Western academy.

While the scope is not intended to be a detailed argument against the epistemological positions of the major Enlightenment figures, David Hume and Immanuel Kant, it will, however, reveal some of the implications of their thought and how they advanced the cause of empirical science, thus promoting the dichotomy. For instance, since empirical science precludes the existence of the supernatural or, more generally, any non-material reality, it set the stage for the decline of theism as the dominant view of the Western world and for the ascendency of its replacement, philosophical naturalism. One of the principal tasks here, then, following Charles Taylor, will be to offer a perspective on how and why the once dominant theistic worldview in the West eventually gave way to a naturalistic worldview that would determine itself to be the exclusive view for securing knowledge and truth.[29] A critical question would certainly be,

---

29   J. Samuel Preus' work, *Explaining Religion,* is a historical study in which he poses the question of the origin of religion (cause and source) to several authors with the goal of showing how "a naturalistic approach to religion achieved paradigmatic status as a new enterprise." It is important to note here that what Preus means by naturalism is that religion is treated as an element of culture without reference to an innate religious sense. He traces this development through a series of historically influential scholars. *Explaining Religion: Criticism and Theory from Bodin to Freud* (Atlanta: Scholars Press, 1996).

how and why did theism fail to adequately counter the work of Hume and Kant?

1.5 Clarifications

Few would deny the accuracy of the assessment of the religion/science relationship described above. Indeed, it appears indisputable that this way of explaining the relationship has achieved paradigmatic status. But as this project will show, to substantiate a distinction in this way is problematic on several levels. Some have explained the distinction between the two categories as natural v. supernatural, or belief in God or gods v. no god. While these distinctions may be valid, they fall short, however, as *the* definitive essence of the religion category. As is commonly understood, not all so-called religions affirm the supernatural or the existence of a God or gods, thus confusing the distinction. Christianity, for example, is contradictory to Buddhism in every possible way yet they both belong to the religion category. More clarification for the categories is needed. If a distinction is made, then there must be a definable difference identified.

Is a definition of religion important?

Although it is often ignored, resolving the religion definition issue is imperative for intelligible inquiry if dialogue is to be fruitful. How does anyone, particularly a scholar, know what to inquire about without a definitive concept to work with? What is the difference between religion and non-religion whether assessed philosophically or culturally? What are the essential differences dividing the two categories? Again, is religion *a thing* that is identifiable? If religion is to be considered a concept, then it must have a unique characteristic, or set of characteristics, that distinguishes it from other concepts. If we say that a religion, minimally, is a set of beliefs and practices, then what is non-religion—a different set of beliefs and practices? It would seem that the two categories consist of two opposing sets of beliefs and practices, while at the same time being formally and functionally alike. If a distinction is made, then the differences must be made clear. For the purposes of this project, fundamental definitions will need to be established, which will be addressed in the next chapter.

A useful definition for the idea of religion is not the only issue that needs to be addressed. Each of these two basic categories represents a multitude of sub-views and all claim to have knowledge and, therefore, truth. The implicit question then that begs to be answered is—which one, if any, has knowledge and truth? Is an answer possible? If the answer is, no, then it does not matter which view is believed. Each view can claim knowledge and truth without any way to have certainty or to resolve differences. How can the claim then be considered knowledge? Without knowledge, choices would lose their significance and be, essentially, meaningless. All meaningful dialogue and argument then cease. On the other hand, if one view can be known to be true, then certainty and meaning are secured. But how that is accomplished needs to be demonstrated. There is much at stake with these questions and to the answers given. In the grandest sense, it is the answer given to the question of meaning and purpose of existence itself.

The privileged view has the burden of proof.

Although the very concept of 'truth' is a problematic issue for today's scholars attempting to remain objective with their research, nonetheless, naturalists believe that they possess knowledge and truth and that it has been acquired objectively. This is what substantiates naturalism's privileged position in the academy. However, along with this claim comes the burden of evidence and proof. But the notion of proof, ironically, is not one that is often addressed by the twentieth century academic ethos. Universities are supposed to be bastions for truth seekers, but the notion of truth is more often explicitly ignored, while unavoidably presupposing some concept of it. For instance, the commonly assumed formulation, especially in the Western academy, is that naturalism is thought to be the stronger position, based on knowledge, and religion the weaker, based on opinion and belief.

Naturalism is assumed to be 'true' and the owner of the exclusive research methodology, which is assumed to be neutral and objective. This point is made manifest by the questions that are asked. Due to its stronger position, science, or rather philosophical naturalism, assumes that the category of religion 'arises' and asks questions such as; where did religion come from, what is the nature of its origin, and why does it exist? In other words, what are the possible causes of views, such as theism, that reject naturalism? How and why is it possible, it is queried, for these alternative views to be believed?

These are the primary concerns of a naturalistic academic approach to religion theory, which assume a privileged role when asking these questions about opposing alternative views. That is, it assumes an authoritative role and perspective when interpreting and explaining other views.[30] It also assumes the validity of the two categories of belief—there is naturalism and then there are the alternative views. From this it would appear that the idea of religion is any view that is contrary to naturalism, perhaps the reason for the difficulty in defining religion. The academy is the place where critical thinking occurs, or ought to occur. Should the academy not also be examining the uncritically held presuppositions, the foundational beliefs, of the privileged view?

Given the perspective of naturalism, the methods of inquiry by eminent religion theorists assume that the idea of religion is somehow derived from nature by natural causes; it is a thing and is explainable just as any other object of critical investigation. So-called religious belief systems are thought to be explainable in either anthropological (E.B. Tylor), psychological (Freud), or sociological (Durkheim) terms.

---

30   Preus develops the idea that "a naturalistic approach to religion achieved paradigmatic status as a new enterprise—not only in the sense of being articulated in thought (as in Hume's "science of man"), but by becoming institutionalized as well...." *Explaining Religion*, xii.

Depending on the interests of the particular theorist, the specific answers to the questions will vary, however. These types of concerns, regularly raised in theory courses in university Religious Studies programs, presuppose a naturalistic perspective.[31] Any affirmation of a reality that transcends a material reality is either dubious or a discoverable product of culture or a projection of the human psyche. The next chapter will discuss several contemporary religion theorists who believe they have the proper way to interpret the idea of religion. What will be evident is that they claim neutral objectivity in their scholarship while uncritically presupposing naturalism, which actually betrays objectivity.

The two categories, while popularly conceived as mutually exclusive, are, nonetheless, unavoidably related as each seeks interpretive power and authority—albeit from their respective differing perspectives. But in keeping with the questioning strategy, it can also be asked, where did this paradigm, this conceptual scheme, come from and why has this type of divide come to be so readily embraced in the West? Are these categories, as presently divided, warranted or is the divide just a thin veil for an Enlightenment ideal that gained favor in order to promote one view, naturalism, over the others? Why should naturalism not be considered just a modern social power construct? To counter these charges, naturalism will need to provide rational proof for its most basic beliefs in order to maintain its privileged role. Without the support of a sound argument, could it be legitimately asked; from whence the origin of naturalism? Why does it exist and how did it arise? If religion arises, does naturalism also arise? The answer given for the origin question depends on the perspective of the questioner and the rational soundness of the respective position.

31   The methodology for the study of the "science of religion" is a much debated topic in academia. See Donald Wiebe's *The Politics of Religious Studies* (New York: Palgrave, 1999). In this work he uses a series of lectures to address the methodological issues between theology and the scientific method. See also the work of historian, Claude Welch, particularly chapter three, "Faith Viewed from Without: The 'Objective' Study of Religious Subjectivity" where he explores the historical development of the application of methodological naturalism in his, *Protestant Thought in the Nineteenth Century, Vol.2* (New Haven: Yale University Press, 1985). Also in the same volume see 110-123 for more discussion on late nineteenth century methodology.

Deconstructing the dichotomy.

The intended ultimate objective for this project will be to deconstruct the prevailing category dichotomy and the understanding of religion that modernity has created. This task will require a reformulation and thereby provide a more accurate and fruitful method by which to divide and classify the world's various systems of belief and practice. As a deconstruction project it will demonstrate specifically how modernity has erroneously produced its particular understanding of the term religion and for what purpose. Once assessed, naturalism, as a belief system, will be shown to have been established on a foundation that cannot be rationally defended. The present conception of religion is unacceptable and, as a construction project, a viable alternative will be offered. Thus, intellectual progress through growth in knowledge and understanding will result.

It will also be demonstrated in the following what each category needs in order to be rationally justified. First principles, that is, the presuppositions and starting point for the reasoning process, need to be rationally proven and not simply dogmatically postulated as self-evident truths in the order of Cartesian 'clear and distinct ideas.' These are the basic beliefs that form the foundation for a belief system. First principles work as presuppositions from which logical inferences are made in order to arrive at meaning and truth.[32] Since a presupposition is ultimate, it is not possible to get behind it to confirm or verify it through additional demonstration. It is one's most basic belief about existence. If it were possible to get behind a presupposition, then something else would be more ultimate and would constitute a more basic principle. As an example, for theism, the presupposition, or basic belief concerning what is ultimate, is a God who is a spirit that is infinite, eternal, and immutable. That such a being exists has not yet been rationally justified, according to naturalists, and is, therefore, rejected as unproven fideistic dogmatism.

---

32   Gangadean, *Philosophical Foundation*, 40-41.

If not the God of theism, what then ultimately exists? Philosophical naturalism postulates the material universe as an alternative. But can matter be proven to be all that exists and all that has ever existed, or can it also only be dogmatically postulated? If it can only be dogmatically postulated, how then can naturalism be considered a stronger, more rational, position than theism? How can it be considered privileged? One's view of the physical world and science will be determined by the answer given to these contradictory presuppositions just described. This is the issue at hand and if it cannot be resolved, then we are left only with skepticism and Nietzsche's 'will to power,' postmodernity's answer.

Late nineteenth and early twentieth century so-called pragmatic philosophy, building on David Hume and empiricism, has dealt with the issue of first principles by denying that knowledge of them is possible. Reason, according to philosophers Hume, Immanuel Kant, and others, cannot grasp a transcendent reality in order to determine such basic things. Continuing that trend, the modern notion of certainty has been challenged by what has been termed, postmodern criticism. The postmodern outlook denies the dichotomy between science and religion by denying the dichotomy between truth and error. Claims to knowledge of truth and error, good and evil, are contextually situated only. Knowledge of ultimate reality from any perspective, theistic or naturalistic, is not possible because reason does not have a rationally justified starting point and, therefore, nothing can be clear to reason. If nothing is clear, then distinctions cannot be made regarding true and false, right and wrong, good and evil, and, therefore, there is no basis for the tension between science and religion. Without objective knowledge, such binaries lose their meaning. Each view pursues its own relative 'truth.'[33] This view, as a postmodern response to the claims of naturalism and theism, will be examined in more detail in what follows.

---

33   See footnote 28 above for works addressing this issue.

1.6 A Brief Sketch of the Project

Following this introduction, five chapters will assess and analyze an aspect of what is being called the modern paradigm and dichotomy with the last chapter including a summary of the project and argument. Chapter two will further explore the tension between the categories and offer workable definitions for the project. It will also demonstrate how naturalism is presupposed in the works of contemporary 'religious studies' scholars. Because the development of the idea of religion is interrelated with the development of science, an historical context tracing the new modern science of the seventeenth century and forward, including its related philosophical foundation, will be established in the second and third chapters.

The third chapter will explore the intellectual developments through this period and show how changes in epistemological thought were instrumental in determining how the physical sciences were understood. Modern science, while having its roots in specific discoveries and theories, took a particular direction as a result of the intellectual climate of the day. Subsequent to the cultural crisis created by the sixteenth-century Protestant Reformation, an environment consisting of questions surrounding the nature of authority, knowledge, reason, and certainty were of central concern. Consequently, the subject of epistemology, 'is knowledge possible' was a formidable question—one to which seventeenth-century philosophy attempted to respond.

Chapter four will sketch the rise and development of Western modernity with particular emphasis on the move from natural theology and philosophy within a Christian theistic framework to a non-theistic philosophy of naturalism. As the new science transformed into a worldview philosophy and gained dominance, the once commanding Christian theistic view declined and was then marginalized and determined irrelevant for dialogue in the public square. Views incommensurate with the new empirical naturalism were categorized, beginning with Christianity, as religion, which would then ultimately become an expanded class and represented by the term, World Religions. These views opposing naturalism, these World Religions, needed their origins, beliefs, and practices interpreted and explained to which religion theorists responded with a new academic discipline—the science of religion. The basic question of David Hume would then need to be addressed, from whence did these belief systems—these religions—arise?

The fifth and sixth chapters will bring this long-standing issue to the present by exploring two contemporary challenges to modernity and its understanding of the religion/science dichotomy. Both will specifically challenge naturalism's claim to exclusive knowledge, however, from different perspectives. The fifth chapter will address the first challenge. It will explain the epistemological strategy of non-foundationalism, the epistemic basis for postmodernity that has challenged the very idea of a foundation for objective knowledge that leads to certainty.

The sixth and final chapter will address the second challenge to the popular religion/science paradigm. It will defend epistemic foundationalism and clarify the need for rational justification for all views claiming knowledge, whether theism or philosophical naturalism, in order to avoid dogmatism. The chapter will also argue that the category and the term, 'religion,' is no longer useful for a consistent and meaningful advancement of human knowledge and understanding. As indicated above, it will be argued that the category and term have been misappropriated by modernity in order to advance a particular epistemology and worldview—a particular philosophy of science/religion.

With the dichotomy deconstructed, the chapter will then develop a radical proposal for better understanding diverse worldviews. It will offer an alternative conceptual scheme that has the potential to avoid the difficulties and connotative baggage associated with the term 'religion' and the resultant theories about origin and nature (e.g. cultural, psychological, social, etc.). The proposed alternative term and concept is the German word, *Weltanschauung* (worldview), which, for starters, is definable, comprehensive, and distinguishable from what it is not. It will be argued that the concept, *Weltanschauung*, in conjunction with basic beliefs, offers a different framework by which to categorize the world's various understandings of reality and show how this can be done. In its most basic sense, worldview will be understood as a set of beliefs that give meaning to one's, or a culture's, experience. It will show how belief systems have analyzable formal structures that allow for grouping according to fundamental beliefs. These beliefs then produce the descriptive data of phenomenology.

2

Religion and Science – The Popular Paradigm

2.1 Two Categories of Belief

THIS CHAPTER WILL explore how a tension developed over the past two centuries between the new science and alternative views resulting in the categories of science and religion. It will illustrate how science evolved into philosophical naturalism and attained a position of prominence over the idea of religion in the academy and is often presupposed in the works of contemporary 'religious studies' scholars. Also, of significance in this chapter, will be to establish workable definitions for achieving a measure of clarity.

The diverse beliefs and practices of people that make up the cultures of the world have provided rich opportunities for scholarly research and discovery—the substance of the social sciences. Western scientific thought, as it gained momentum and expression in the eighteenth century Enlightenment era, recognized this diversity and sought to organize and categorize views different from its own, which would come to be understood as religion and, eventually, world religions.

Religion scholar, Wilfred C. Smith, chronicles the evolution of the Latin term *religio* from its earliest usage to the present and argues for an approach to the idea of religion as an individual personal piety. Smith considers religion to be notoriously difficult to define and any attempt as an artificial construct and ultimately a fruitless exercise.[1] The category of religion, which has been understood at least since the early eighteenth century to consist of distinct and explainable belief systems and practices that can be differentiated from non-religion, arguably arose from controversies of modernity in England.

Historian, Peter Harrison, in his Gifford Lectures and subsequent book, *'Religion' and the Religions in the English Enlightenment*, elaborated convincingly on this theme. In this work on the rise of the idea of religion from the Enlightenment forward, Harrison argues that "[t]he origins of the modern idea of religion can be traced to the Enlightenment. This study shows how the concepts 'religion' and 'the religions' arose out of controversies in seventeenth and eighteenth-century England. The birth of 'the religions', conceived to be sets of beliefs and practices, enabled the establishment of a new science of religion in which the various 'religions' were studied and impartially compared." Commenting on Wilfred C. Smith, Harrison states, "[i]t is Smith's contention that during the age of reason the name 'religion' was given to external aspects of the religious life, to systems of practices. Whereas in the Middle Ages the concern of the Christian West had been with faith—a 'dynamic of the heart'—in the seventeenth-century attention shifted to the impersonal and objective 'religion.' Increasingly this term came to be an outsider's description of a dubious theological enterprise."[2] Harrison further examines this process

---

1   For a detailed background explanation on this point, see Smith's, *The Meaning and End of Religion* (New York: New American Library, A Mentor Book, 1962) 16-22; 34-44. Thomas Tweed also notes that "religion is not a native term; it is a term created by scholars for their intellectual purposes and therefore is theirs to define," *Crossing and Dwelling: A Theory of Religion* (Cambridge MA: Harvard University Press, 2006) 33.

2   Peter Harrison, *'Religion' and the Religions in the English Enlightenment* (New York: Cambridge University Press, 1990) 1-2. See also Tomoko Masuzawa who traces the advent of

of objectification, or reification, of religious faith, focusing particularly on the English contribution to the ideation of 'religion' and 'the religions.'

The scientific view produced by modernity has been variously characterized by terms such as materialism, metaphysical naturalism, philosophical naturalism, or simply, naturalism, and emphasized a perspective ultimately and exclusively based on the deliverables of the physical sciences. While each of these terms is associated with modernity in some way, naturalism will be the term most commonly used in this project and intended to be synonymous with the others. This new developing view functioned as a non-theistic alternative to the prevailing Christian theism.

As the naturalistic view progressed and the beliefs and practices of other cultures were explored in the nineteenth century, Christian theism became part of a larger general category and called religion. The religion category functioned as modernity's means to separate all other perspectives on reality from the naturalistic position, thus forming a dichotomy, or contradiction, between two mutually exclusive categories of belief. A polarity between theism and naturalism was the result. James Thrower, in his work on historic atheism, emphasizes this point and makes the following comment;

There is, however, a way of looking at and interpreting events in the world, whose origins, as I hope to show, can be seen as early as the beginnings of speculative thought itself, and which I shall call naturalistic, that is atheistic *per se*, in the sense that it is incompatible with any and every form of supernaturalism.[3]

Non-theism, as an alternative to theism, established itself more clearly as a viable worldview during this time. It is now generally defined by the

---

world religions in her, *The Invention of World Religions* (The University of Chicago Press: Chicago, 2005) and Talal Asad's, *Genealogies of Religion* (Baltimore: The Johns Hopkins University Press, 1993).

3   James Thrower, *Western Atheism: A Short History* (Amherst, NY: Prometheus Books, 2000) 3-4.

achievements of the empirical sciences, thus distinguishing and distancing it from the so-called religious views. As a result, the modern West has been forced to come to grips with how to understand the relationship between the ostensibly antithetical classical and medieval representations of what has come to be called a religious understanding of the world, particularly as expressed by Christian theism, and the new modern alternative outlook characterized by a progressive, materialistic science.

Thrower identifies the rise of the secularist attitude in Western Europe in the Middle Ages with the dissociation of faith and reason and the limitation placed upon the scope of reason. This, then, gave rise to the development of physical science as an exclusive and comprehensive way of looking at the world. He also notes the dynamic in naturalistic atheism as having "a consistency which makes it a genuine and alternative way of looking at the world from that which has inspired the religious believer."[4]

Christian theism, the predominant view with which modernity had to deal, was considered to be an entity having certain characteristics, such as belief in a transcendent, supernatural reality, which could be identified and placed in a separate generic category. Such a view was considered by some to be incompatible with and even in opposition to the emerging current of naturalistic ideas gaining momentum in Britain and Europe. It was soon considered a hindrance to intellectual advancement and knowledge.[5] The term 'religion,' having already been a part of Christian self-descriptive language, was applied as a general label of classification. Christian theism, as a belief system, acquired the status of a religion and, as such, became rising naturalism's chief dialogue interlocutor and contender for primacy in the West.

Due to the dominant position of Christian theism in the West historically, this project focuses primarily on it as the representative for the category of religion, the primary interest of modernity and naturalism.

4   Thrower, *Western Atheism*, 3.

5   Thrower, *Western Atheism*, 96-116. See also, John Hedley Brooke, *Science and Religion: Some Historical Perspectives* (Cambridge, UK: Cambridge University Press, 1991) Chapter 7.

The naturalistic view, as a distinct entity and category with its own identifiable characteristics that were separate from Christian theism, became,
and continues to be, the non-religious view. This alternative view, the
non-religious and identified with science, developed somewhat historically parallel with the idea of religion. Thus, we have two developing frameworks of belief and practice, religion and non-religion, each a product
of Western modernity. The historical evolution and interrelationship of
these two entities will be explored in the next two chapters, but first some
comments on the perceived tension between them.

2.2 Category Tension

The idea of religion as it has developed is an on-going topic of dialogue
and oftentimes tension over its place in the modern and, what has come to
be called, the secular world. In response, a relatively new field of inquiry
devoted specifically to issues related to the relationship between religion
and science has gained interest and momentum in recent years. Scholars
are frequently challenged with questions about how these two diverse perspectives should relate, if at all. Are these different ways of understanding
the world actually in conflict with each other or are they two mutually
exclusive disciplines of inquiry with no need for conflict or intersection?
While the relationship issue has been a debated matter for at least the
past two hundred years, several views have prevailed depicting the two
as mortal enemies, friendly allies, or somewhere in between.[6] Most of
the dialogue has been framed in these terms. However, as historian John
Hedley Brooke has noted,

> Popular generalizations about that relationship, whether couched
> in terms of war or peace, simply do not stand up to serious in-

---

6   For a detailed discussion of the various views on this relationship see David C. Lindberg and
     Ronald L. Numbers, eds., *God and Nature: Historical Essays on the Encounter Between Chris-
     tianity and Science* (Berkeley and Los Angeles, CA: University of California Press, 1986). See
     also *The Oxford Handbook of Religion and Science*, eds., Philip Clayton and Zachary Simpson
     (Oxford: Oxford University Press, 2006).

vestigation. There is no such thing as *the* relationship between science and religion. It is what different individuals and communities have made of it in a plethora of different contexts. Not only has the problematic interface between them shifted over time, but there is also a high degree of artificiality in abstracting the science and the religion of earlier centuries to see how they were related.[7]

As Brooke indicates, a normative prescription of how these two entities are to relate does not exist. Perhaps this is due to the fact that much of the dialogue has been largely undertaken without adequate assessment of the presuppositions held by each perspective. Additionally, the historical context is so important for properly understanding these two terms that attempts to reify them result in only artificial definitions. Brooke further notes that it would be a mistake to do this, "as if they could be completely abstracted from the social contexts in which those concerns and endeavors took their distinctive forms."[8] Conceptions of the natural world and how it is to be conceived and explained have been an integral part of human history, especially in its social and political application of scientific innovations. It is therefore imperative that the specific use of the terms, religion and science, be understood in their historical context as accurately as possible.

The assumption, of course, in all of these relationship perspectives is that this inquiry has value and an ongoing dialogue of some type is worth

---

7   John Hedley Brooke, *Science and Religion: Some Historical Perspectives* (Cambridge, UK: Cambridge University Press, 1991) 321. Brooke goes on to say that "Part of what was meant by natural philosophy in the seventeenth century involved a discussion of God's relationship to nature. Religious beliefs could operate within science, proving presupposition and sanction as well as regulating the discussion of method. They also informed attitudes toward new conceptions of nature, influencing the process of theory selection. In the eighteenth and nineteenth centuries, despite vigorous attempts to separate scientific and religious discourse, the meaning attributed to scientific innovations continued to be reflected in the often conflicting social, religious, and political uses to which they were put." 321.

8   Brooke, *Science and Religion,* 8.

the effort. A recent symposium sponsored by the International Society for Science and Religion focused on the importance of continued dialogue between the two disciplines. The end product of the work was a book entitled, *Why the Science and Religion Dialogue Matters*. In it, most of the contributors reflect the conviction "that the dialogue between science and religion is of wide social and cultural importance." Emphasizing this point, Fraser Watts, one of the editors and a contributor, comments that "religion and science each proceed best when they're pursued in dialogue with the other, and also that our fragmented and divided world order would benefit more from a stronger dialogue between science and religion."[9]

Implicit in these statements, at least minimally, is a perceived separation and tension between religion and science that many believe needs to be addressed in order to achieve some kind of cultural accord. The term, tension, may be too strong or too weak for some, but if not tension, then definitely a chasm that separates in some way according to the common conception.

However, on the surface, to even speak of tension and separation seems odd if religion and science are understood in a straightforward manner. For instance, in a fundamental sense, religion, as delineated above, is often thought of as belief in the existence of a transcendent reality. It does not typically deny the existence of the physical world (in the West), but affirms a spiritual in addition to a material reality.

Science, on the other hand, also in a fundamental sense, consists of counting, weighing, and measuring the data gathered by exploring the physical world. Fundamentally, it is a descriptive and not a prescriptive process. Philosopher, W. V. Quine, puts it this way; "[w]hat makes for science is system, whatever the subject. And what makes for system is the judicious application of logic. Science is thus a fruit of rational investiga-

---

9   Fraser Watts and Kevin Dutton, eds., *Why the Science and Religion Dialogue Matters* (Philadelphia, PA: Templeton Foundation Press, 2006) vii. The International Society for Science and Religion was organized in 2001 and is similar in purpose to the acclaimed Scottish Gifford Lectures where the focus is more on natural theology.

RELIGION AND SCIENCE

tion."[10] For science, whether a transcendent reality exists or not does not seem to be a primary concern for gathering data and producing fruit. The two appear to be complementary, as they were thought to be prior to the mid-nineteenth century.[11] So why the separation and/or the tension? The tension arises at a different level, and in part, due to the ambiguity surrounding these two terms. It exists because the meaning and significance of the terms, religion and science, are embedded in a larger belief system, a worldview, or what some have termed an ideological construct. Belief systems provide the framework by which the data of experience and science are interpreted and explained. For meaning and significance, data needs to be interpreted—what does it mean? As comprehensive views of the world are formed and adherents become more consciously aware of their own beliefs, the differences between one view and another become more apparent. The terms religion and science have been transformed from their original meanings as *religio* and *scientia* and have become substantive elements of comprehensive worldviews. As Brooke noted, they become contextualized.

Religion and science, as presently understood, are separated not because they are fundamentally antithetical to each other, but because they have become embedded in, and identified with, worldviews that perceive,

10   W. V. Quine, J. S. Ullian, *The Web of Belief*, 2ⁿᵈ ed. (New York: McGraw-Hill, 1978) 3.

11   Historian, Theodore Dwight Bozeman, explains in his detailed historical work on Protestants and science that "antebellum America, marked by a lively and growing interest in natural science and evangelical Protestantism, widely nurtured the comfortable assumption that science *and* religion, Baconianism *and* the Bible, were harmonious enterprises cooperating toward the same ultimate ends." Nineteenth century American Protestantism desired "to secure a broad harmonization of science with religion" and viewed Francis Bacon as a pious evangelical believer. This attitude "reflected a 'doxological' view of natural science, which styled the scientist a worshipful elucidator of the Divine creation. The conception of research as praise rested on a long tradition of scientific piety and concentrated on manifestations in nature of providential design, order, and care." He goes on to say, "the emergence of the issue in this predominant form—science versus religion—was a new and uncoveted experience for orthodox apologists. They had regarded their previous skirmishes with impious science as passing collisions that did not endanger the centraledifice of the holy alliance" *Protestants in an Age of Science: The Baconian Ideal and Antebellum American Religious Thought* (Chapel Hill: The University of North Carolina Press, 1977) xv, 161, 168.

interpret, and explain experience, the nature of the world and reality, differently. So-called religions offer an interpretation in the form of a metanarrative that explains the meaning and nature of the world and reality. Included in that interpretation is a view of the physical world and the exploration and explanation of it.

For science, on the other hand, the gathering of so-called 'neutral' data does not stop there, but includes more. To use the oft-quoted phrase, *all data are theory-laden*. Like religion, the additional component for science, or rather philosophical naturalism, is that of interpretation, which precedes theory and explanation. Physical data alone are inconsequential—there is no meaning, and, therefore, must be incorporated into a larger framework that provides a basis from which to interpret the meaning and significance of the data. Philosopher of science and religion, Ian Barbour, has aptly noted, "[e]xpectations and conceptual commitments influence perceptions, both in everyday life and in science."[12] As rational beings, humans need meaning and significance in order to understand experience, and interpretation is part of the rational process that provides it. So, religion and science (philosophical naturalism), both interpret and explain the data of experience, however, begin the process from different basic beliefs. More on this point will be discussed below.

Naturalism then, in addition to gathering data, also interprets the data (what does it mean) and develops its own metanarrative (e.g. Darwinism) that, like so-called religion, explains the nature and meaning of the data, which reflects basic beliefs about reality itself. It is, then, also a philosophy—and thus the more descriptive term, philosophical naturalism. In other words, philosophical naturalism, the worldview that has come to represent modern science, interprets and explains and, therefore, formally functions like a religion. Both are involved in interpretation, but affirm something different to be the most basic, or ultimate reality upon which the system rests. Each has a different starting point. Each interprets

---

12   Ian Barbour, *Myths, Models and Paradigms: A Comparative Study in Science and Religion* (New York: Harper & Row Publishers, 1974) 95.

and explains in light of its most basic judgment about what is ultimately real—a metaphysical judgment.

Whether explicitly acknowledged or not, naturalism makes, of necessity, a metaphysical statement. It cannot avoid it in spite of the postmodern argument to the contrary. It makes a metaphysical judgment when it affirms that reality is material existence only. A noteworthy statement on this is one by Carl Sagan, "the Cosmos is all that is or was or ever will be."[13] So-called religion also affirms the existence of a material reality, but additionally affirms the existence of a non-material (spiritual) reality. The two categorical views, religion and naturalism, formally function the same, however, hold metaphysically opposed basic beliefs.

While the tension may not have been fully apparent by the mid-nineteenth century, as modernity matured and science transformed into a worldview based on philosophical naturalism, the separation and tension between the two perspectives became more pronounced. Awareness of metaphysical differences increased. Philosopher, Alvin Plantinga, considers this point to be the major issue between religion and science. He does not contrast religion and science as such, but puts it more specifically, as does this present work, by framing it as worldview v. worldview, or theism v. philosophical naturalism. He identifies the worldview tension as "where the conflict really lies," and as one of our culture's biggest debates.[14]

When understood in this way, these two worldviews are contradictory to each other, which then demands explanation. They are not just contrary, but are contradictory. Contradictory propositions cannot both be true and cannot both be false. Of logical necessity, one must be false and the other must be true. Arguments are made by each position and offered as evidence to justify belief.

---

13 Carl Sagan, *Cosmos*, (New York: Random House, 2013) 1.

14 Alvin Plantinga, *Where the Conflict Really Lies* (Oxford: Oxford University Press, 2011). British philosopher of science, John Lennox, also makes the point that the conflict is not between science and religion, but "the real conflict is between two diametrically opposed worldviews; naturalism and theism. They inevitably collide." *God's Undertaker: Has Science Buried God?* (Oxford: Lion Hudson plc, 2009) 28-29.

Due to the different beliefs regarding what is ultimate, the tension is often recognized as such and sides are taken forming a separation, or dichotomy, between these two categories of belief. While this work addresses the reason for the tension, it does, however, frame it differently than the typical discourse. The approach will explore a more basic issue, the foundational presupposition of each category, which is seldom addressed. That is, science (philosophical naturalism) and so-called religion have come to be understood as two separate ways of viewing reality, which then constitutes the two different categories of belief. Each belief system, or category, has a foundational belief that separates one from the other. It is this basic belief, or presupposition, that makes them contradictory.

Much has been assumed in the making of these two categories and the presuppositions need to be identified. Whether the basis for the category distinction as presently understood is valid or not needs to be assessed conclusively. For instance, what are the most basic beliefs of each category regarding what is ultimately eternal and what is the essential difference between them and support for their claims? Each category claims 'to know' and to have exclusive knowledge about the ultimate nature of reality. One category claims that matter only is eternal and the other that a non-material spirit is the only eternal reality. But can each respective category rationally support its claims or can they merely dogmatically postulate belief and opinion?

The commonly accepted view affirms that the philosophical naturalism representing science can claim knowledge, and religion cannot. But can this claim be demonstrated or has it just been assumed to be so? If the claim of knowledge by naturalism can be demonstrated to be false or, as postmodernity maintains, unknowable whether true of false, should the academy, for the sake of accurate scholarship, re-evaluate its approach to the relationship between religion and science?

It should be clear that the tension is not between so-called religion and science, but between the worldviews of theism and philosophical naturalism. As mentioned above, while the relationship between science and theism has been a debated topic, if a poll were taken today the average person, both inside and outside of academia, would most likely side with those who sense a tension.

Militaristic adjectives such as conflict, warfare, battle, and weapons have been common terminology in discourse describing the relationship since the late nineteenth century and continues to today. Given that each affirms a different conception of ultimate reality, it would be hard to see it in any other way. If understood from the conservative theist's perspective, it would be hard to conceive of the relationship from the end of the nineteenth century to the present as anything other than one of conflict. Since this project addresses the rise of philosophical naturalism and the marginalization of theism and, therefore, *prima facie* confrontational, the attention here will be directed at the basis for the conflict between the two.

At this point an effort to establish at least a minimal definition of the idea of religion and science to better differentiate the two is in order. Without an understanding of the fundamental difference between what is presently called religion and science, it is impossible to draw conclusions regarding the relationship. What this will reveal is that science, like religion, is an ambiguous idea and must be understood from within the hermeneutic of Western modernity. Additionally, if the category distinction promoted by modernity cannot be rationally substantiated, it can then be nothing more than a convenient social construct of Western modernity. Some of the intellectual developments that have more or less consciously informed and shaped all academic fields of inquiry, including the field of religious studies, will also be explored. This category tension forms the backdrop for what follows.

2.3 The Idea of Religion

After using the term religion numerous times above and discussing the tension surrounding it, it is significant to note again that today the term, religion, is considered undefinable by many religion scholars and has led to much confusion as to what religion is and just as important, what it is not.

But is it necessary to define the term? Anthropologist, Talal Asad, has commented that "there cannot be a universal definition of religion, not only because its constituent elements and relationships are historically specific, but because that definition is itself the historic product of discursive processes."[15] In other words, any attempt at definition would need to be contextualized. As Brooke also noted above, the historical context is significant for understanding the idea of religion. What is meant by these scholars is that the term, as it is popularly understood, cannot be universalized. But the attempt continues. Arguably, additional confusion has been largely due to the efforts of religion theorists to negotiate in and around the dichotomy in question without identifying their own presuppositions. To persist in using the term without an understanding of what it is, is to perpetuate the confusion. Some kind of workable definition seems imperative.

A term that cannot be accurately defined presents its own set of problems, one being that it cannot be a concept. A concept allows for differentiation from what it is not by getting to the term's essential meaning. The essence of something is identified by isolating the distinctive qualities that all members of a class and only members of that class always have. At present, the term religion does not allow this. As a result, many textbooks on the subject address, albeit reluctantly, a series of questions such as the following, but without a clear resolution. How are religions identified and what are their essential components? Do some beliefs and practices constitute a religion while others do not? Are all humans religious or are only some religious? How does a religious understanding of the world differ from a non-religious one? What is religious knowledge and what is religious belief?

Within the context of the current understanding, these analytical types of questions can be answered with only a relative degree of accuracy,

---

15   Asad, *Genealogies*, 29.

if at all. Without a workable, sustainable definition that allows for at least a minimal consensus on the fundamentals makes a distinctive objective for religious studies virtually impossible. For instance, how do religious studies differ from cultural studies, anthropological studies, philosophical studies, political studies, theological studies, or scientific studies for that matter? Granted, there may be overlap and shared terms in all of these, but what is the essential difference between these disciplines and so-called religion? Some would argue that there is no difference and that so-called religions are nothing more than socially constructed ideologies that need to be researched as cultural phenomena.

Religion scholars have struggled with this most challenging demand for definition and its place in intellectual inquiry. For religion to be a concept it must have specific characteristics that all members and only members of the class 'religion' have in common. And as just mentioned, this allows for the idea of religion to be differentiated from what it is not. It is at this point that comprehensive definitions have stumbled. Consequently, many religion scholars accept as incontestable that the term, religion, is undefinable, considering it simply a collective name, and opt for something like William James' view that religion "consists in the belief that there is an unseen order, and that our supreme good lies in harmoniously adjusting ourselves thereto."[16] But this statement is exceedingly broad, contributing to and illustrating the problem.

The difficulty here is that this expression is so broad that it could conceivably include all views, including naturalism. A naturalist may propose that "our supreme good lies in harmoniously adjusting ourselves" to the "unseen order" inherent in natural selection and the survival of the fittest. But if that is the intention of the statement, then the dichotomy would lose its meaning and dissolve. All views could be included in only one category, the religion category, or the non-religion category. If all is religion, then none is religion. But this, most likely, was not James' inten-

---

16   Quoted in Lewis Hopfe, Mark Woodward, *Religions of the World*, 8ᵗʰ ed. (Upper Saddle River, NJ: Prentiss-Hall, 2001) 5.

tion at all. However, an assertion like this when not clearly crafted loses its intended meaning. Though it does indicate the difficulty in identifying a common characteristic that allows for a comprehensive definition for all that is typically called religion. But perhaps, it is not as difficult as it may at first appear.

Expressing a possible cause for this difficulty is Jonathan Z. Smith in his now famous statement already quoted above, "[t]here is no data for religion.....Religion has no independent existence apart from the academy." If James' vagueness and Smith's judgment are correct, the dichotomy then collapses—the current paradigm is flawed. This, it will be shown, is the logical consequence and needs to be advanced further.

Taking a similar position, religion historian, Timothy Fitzgerald makes a strong case that the idea of religion has been misconceived. He argues that there are either theological studies or cultural studies. The current idea of religion, he says, is that it "indicates some reality that is not already covered by 'society' and 'culture', that religion is something over and above and additional to society and culture. Outside of a specific theological claim, this implication is, I believe, a fallacy."[17] He goes on to say that many scholars hope to employ religion as an analytical concept, to distinguish religious institutions and values from non-religious ones. But, to do this, he contends, is a futile quest because "it either operates as a theological concept, though one disguised by the so-called science of religion; or alternatively it operates at a very general level of meaning that makes it virtually indistinguishable from 'culture.'"[18] He summarizes his thesis well with this statement:

[T]he more the researcher distances himself or herself from the explicit or implicit theological domination of 'religion', adopting for example sociological or anthropological critical perspectives,

---

17   Timothy Fitzgerald, *The Ideology of Religious Studies* (New York: Oxford University Press, 2000) 222.

18   Fitzgerald, *Ideology,* 225.

the more irrelevant the concept of religion will become, except as an ideological construct of western and western-dominated societies from which the scholar has progressively freed him or herself and that itself requires critical analysis.[19]

Both J. Z. Smith and Fitzgerald reject the notion that the idea of religion has a trans-cultural essence—that it is something that can be isolated from cultural studies. The points they make strongly challenge the status of the idea of religion as a separate category of study. As a result, to identify religion as *sui generis*, a thing in itself and a separate category for inquiry, is a misguided endeavor. Some attempt to find a characteristic, or set of characteristics, that all of the diverse so-called religious views have in common. But Smith and Fitzgerald, as well as others, argue that they are searching in vain. Rather, cultures and their institutions and practices reflect the beliefs and values of agents making choices, personally and collectively.

Contrary to those like Smith and Fitzgerald who want to reduce religion to a more basic discipline, earlier scholars, like Mircea Eliade and Rudolf Otto, contended that religion discourse cannot be reduced to any other form of discourse because it is itself a basic discipline—it is *sui generis*. That is, the idea of religion exists universally; it has an essence and is identifiable as distinct from all other types of inquiry. There is such a thing as 'religious' phenomena, they argue, and it is a part of the human experience—it is part of human nature.

A classic argument for *sui generis* religion has been the argument from the *argumentum e consensus gentium*, the general consent of mankind, or from the Protestant Reformer, John Calvin's, *sensus divinitatis*, a universal sense of deity in all humans. The idea here is that within the human consciousness is an intuitive awareness of the 'sacred' (Eliade), the 'holy' (Otto), and of a transcendent God (Calvin). This intuitive awareness then qualifies as a 'religious' awareness.[20] Advocates of the *sui generis* idea argue

---

19   Fitzgerald, *Ideology*, 8

20   See chapter six for an alternative understanding of this idea.

that religion is something that is unique in its characteristics and this uniqueness needs to be researched and studied.

If religion has an essence, then it must be a concept and have a defining quality that all members of the class 'religion' share. It must have a universal, identifiable, nature. A plethora of ideas, such as the 'sacred,' the 'holy,' or the sense of deity have been offered as 'religious' phenomena and as *the* common and defining characteristic to give religion a unique status for inquiry. But what is the 'sacred' or the 'holy'? How is it determined and identified? Is sacredness and holiness discovered in human nature or is it arbitrarily determined by a particular cultural context or belief perspective?

These ideas of the sacred or the holy, however, presuppose beliefs about human nature that must be clearly stated and analyzed. The notions of 'sacredness,' 'holiness,' and the *sensus divinitatis* (innate awareness of God), are, as Fitzgerald argues, theological concepts and must be understood in light of the basic belief of theism. The discussion is then pushed back into the area of metaphysics, first principles, and the essence of human nature, which will be addressed in subsequent chapters.

Putting the *sui generis* issue aside for now, the point can be made that even without a clear definition, the idea of religion is still applied to varied and contradictory belief systems, which then form a category of belief. What, then, holds these disparate views together? What is the common denominator, the common ground between them? This gets to the issue addressed by the scholars noted above. There is no commonality that can be identified as a trans-cultural object in need of discovery and investigation without presupposing a more basic belief concerning essences.

Smith and Fitzgerald have challenged the idea of religion as a separate entity that stands above the ordinary workings of culture. Rather, they see it as a subcategory of culture and as an ideological totalizing concept for analyzing the diverse values and strategies of power inherent within various cultures and societies. Works in anthropology and sociology are misleading when they suggest that they are about the 'religious' experience of a particular culture. They are really attempts, says Fitzgerald, "to study the institutionalized values of specific social groups, the different ways in which values are symbolically represented, and the relation of those values and symbolic representations to power and other aspects of social organization."[21]

Variously understood as a theological, sociological, anthropological, psychological, or broadly cultural phenomenon, the idea of religion has managed to survive as well as elude a clarifying definition. Numerous attempts at comprehensiveness have been offered in order to delimit the idea. Nonetheless, this effort has been met with little success. The lack of an agreed upon definition has caused much perplexity and tension regarding how to understand the relationship between the idea of religion as it relates to the physical and social sciences. Consequently, the popular religion/science dichotomy is perpetuated.

So, the question continues to be asked, or avoided; what is this thing called religion and what does it do? To ask David Hume's question, how and why did it arise? Or, did it? Is it innate, an integral aspect of human nature? These are fair questions that have been asked historically and have captivated the creative imaginations of the social sciences.

So, it does not seem to be asking too much to demand a working definition. If there is not a workable definition, then how does the scholar know what has purportedly arisen? The answer may be cloaked in irony. Perhaps it is imbedded in the worldview of modernity and is obvious. While a definition of religion from within the religion category may be impossible due to the diversity of views, modernity's naturalism, however, easily defines religion as any belief system that is incommensurate with its own, which is essentially what modernity has done.

For modernity, religion equals non-naturalism. If naturalism is rejected, then the specifics, the distinctive features, of the alternative views

---

21   Fitzgerald, *Ideology*, 12

really do not matter. For instance, Freud's *The Future of an Illusion*, or more recently, Pascal Boyer's, *Religion Explained*, each operates from an explicitly naturalistic perspective and framework. They each presuppose a naturalistic frame of reference; the privileged view attempting to apply a naturalistic methodology for answering questions regarding the cause and origin of alternative views—the so-called religions. What is apparent is that the divide between so-called religion and non-religion has already been presupposed, implying, at least minimally, some sort of definition, which enables one view to be separated from others.

It should be clear at this point that naturalists understand alternative views to be either a psychologically or socially constructed category. It should also be apparent that what is called religion consists of various belief systems that can be understood, at least minimally, by what they affirm to be true and by what they do. They attempt to interpret and explain a conception of reality, essentially how the world works, which includes the assorted practices associated with each. The common characteristic of the diverse views at the most basic level is that they all seek to make sense out of human experience. That is, they describe, interpret, and explain experience in order to maximize the meaning of it, and particular beliefs that form a system are what makes that happen. It should also be clear that, similarly, naturalism is also a belief system that describes, interprets, and explains the nature of reality along with its various ways of practice and, therefore, also seeks to make sense out of human experience.

The formal features, structure, and function of diverse belief systems are alike, but with different basic beliefs. That is, each belief system consists of, whether explicitly stated or uncritically presupposed, a metaphysic, an epistemology, and an ethic. The belief categories of naturalism and so-called religion are similar in that each attempt to interpret and explain the meaning and significance of existence and the human experience of it. Each view inferentially derives from its basic beliefs an interpretation and explanation of the data of existence and experience. In other words, both philosophical naturalism and so-called religion construct systems of interrelated beliefs and propositions that serve to interpret and explain the nature of the world so as to make sense of it. Formally, structurally, and functionally, they are the same.

So, at the most basic level, naturalism and the idea of religion are the same. As one philosopher of religion, Surrendra Gangadean, explains it, "religion is the belief or set of beliefs one uses to give meaning to one's experience....since all give meaning to experience, all are religious."[22] William James' attempt at definition, unwittingly, came to the same conclusion. All belief systems attempt to do the same thing. Once again, if all is religion, then none is religion. When understood in this way, the term 'religion' loses its distinctive and definitive characteristics and is, therefore, debatable whether it qualifies as a concept. It loses its meaning. All of the world's diverse belief systems then qualify as religion.

Whether so-called religion or naturalism, belief systems are constructed for the purpose of giving meaning to human experience. This includes determining the significance and meaning of data gathered from the physical world—what is typically called science. Inherent in the respective systems are beliefs concerning the nature of ultimate reality, how that reality is known, and how life ought to be lived. Sam Harris reflects on the relationship between beliefs and practice with his comment, "[y]our beliefs define your vision of the world; they dictate your behavior; they determine your emotional responses to other human beings."[23] Beliefs and practice are causally connected and cannot be separated.

---

22   Gangadean, *Philosophical Foundation*, 104. Gangadean states, "The definition of religion as an attempt to state the meaning of a term is bound up with one's larger framework of meaning, i.e., one's worldview. That is to say, one's definition of religion reflects one's religion (meaning framework) held more or less consciously and consistently. Insofar as one is not consistently skeptical and given to nihilism, common ground remains. There are commonly accepted examples of religion (Hinduism, Buddhism, Confucianism, Judaism, Christianity, Islam) from which common features of religion may be identified. Belief in a higher power is not a common feature of all of these, but giving meaning to one's experience in light of one's basic belief (true for both theism and atheism/secular humanism/naturalism) is common to all of these religions." 222, FN7.

23   Harris, *End of Faith*, 12.

If all belief systems are formally and functionally the same and develop for the purpose of producing meaning, then, as Gangadean has stated, all views are essentially 'religious.' If all views are essentially religious, then the term 'religion' could easily be replaced with the term 'worldview.' Perhaps the term, worldview (*Weltanschauung*), is better suited as a general category to capture the world's belief systems. It is more comprehensive and more inclusive. Naturalism and religion would then be subsumed by a larger, singular, category heading—worldview. All belief systems, whether naturalism or so-called religion, interpret and explain existence and, therefore, constitute a view of the world.

The points just made address what belief systems fundamentally are and what they fundamentally do. The notion of 'meaningfulness' is the common denominator for all belief systems (religions/worldviews). All beliefs and belief systems, whether naturalism or so-called religion, function and are structured to achieve the same end—coherence and meaning. And as will be shown in what follows, the test for meaning is the consistent use of reason.[24] Beliefs are meaningful when they are consistent with each other, including the most basic belief, and do not violate the laws of thought—they are not contradictory.

With the 'definition' of religion just discussed, the popular paradigm, the two categories of science and religion, collapses and the discussion shifts. The focus is now on a single category consisting of a multitude of belief systems that are structured in such a way as to achieve meaningfulness. But even with only a single category the question of differentiation still remains. Can the multitude of views in the single category still be grouped separately? How are they different? Some may argue that the popular divide is still valid because no substantive change has been produced. One view, naturalism, is still based on reason and knowledge and the others are not, it is claimed. This claim, however, still needs to be critically evaluated. The challenge to the popular paradigm and to naturalism

---

24   Gangadean, *Philosophical Foundation*, 9.

as privileged is not quite complete. The first step was to clarify the issue of definition with respect to structure, function, and meaning, and the second is to address the claim to knowledge and privilege, which is to follow.

While the structure and function for all religions, or belief systems, is the same, the content, or belief particulars, are not. This same critique would apply within the so-called religion category as well. The respective basic beliefs of each view within the religion category are significantly different and even contradictory. Each view holds a different belief regarding what is ultimately real (eternal). That is, there are opposing beliefs with respect to what ultimately exists. Keep in mind that this whole issue of religion/science and worldview is over differences regarding which way is the correct way to understand existence. Moreover, the main difference in the various views is not primarily found in the familiar notion that one view believes in the supernatural and the other does not, as is commonly believed. Some views considered religious, such as Buddhism, affirm a non-material ultimate reality, but not necessarily a supernatural reality. It is at the most basic level of belief, beliefs about what ultimately exists and has always existed, that differences in worldviews ought to be critically assessed. When this is done, the two popular categories dissolve allowing for a new, more objective and comprehensive, scheme.

As an example, naturalism (science) and Hinduism (religion) oppose each other in the popular paradigm. However, when their most basic belief about existence is examined they fall into the same belief category. But. how can that be, it may be asked? Both views believe that something is eternal (our most basic belief) rather than nothing, and both views believe that 'all' that exists is eternal. They differ, however, on what it is that ultimately exists, which is an inferred and less basic belief. Naturalism believes that all that exists is eternal and that it is matter, whereas Hinduism believes that all that exists is eternal and that it is spirit, or non-matter. They both, however, affirm that what ultimately exists is eternal. What is significant here is that they are in the same category at the most basic level.

The question of existence and eternality, as well as a new proposal for dividing belief systems, will be discussed in more detail in chapter six. In that chapter all three options regarding what is eternal will be examined—*all* is eternal, *none* is eternal, and *some* is eternal (some is not eternal).[25] Every worldview, functioning as an ideological concept, affirms explicitly or implicitly a belief about what is most ultimate and its adherents bear responsibility for the rational justification of that belief.

2.4 Explanation, Presuppositions, and Privilege

At this point it is becoming more clear that the idea of religion and non-religion is a fabrication of modernity. Modernity promotes a worldview grounded in a particular interpretation of the data of science and experience. Modernity's understanding of alternative, opposing views is embedded in the worldview of modernity. How alternative views are interpreted and explained is determined in light of the interpreter's most basic belief about what ultimately exists. Interpreting and explaining is not a neutral, objective enterprise. As an example, two renowned contemporary historians of religion demonstrate how interpreting and explaining reveals uncritically held presuppositions, which reflect a particular worldview and belief about the nature of existence.

In his work, *Explaining Religion*, J. Samuel Preus, presupposes the validity of the dichotomy in question.[26] He traces several significant religion theorists, such as Bodin, Vico, Hume, Durkheim, and Freud, with the intent to show how each accounts for, in Preus' estimation, "the key issue—that of origins" (cause and source) that eventually produced the naturalistic paradigm for the interpretation of religion.[27]

---

25 Gangadean develops these options in detail in his work *Philosophical Foundation*.

26 J. Samuel Preus, *Explaining Religion: Criticism and Theory from Bodin to Freud* (Atlanta: Scholars Press, 1996).

27 Preus, *Explaining*, ix, xxi.

From the work of these theorists, he articulates how the development of a modern naturalistic approach to the study of religion superseded a theological approach. He argues that a theological approach to understanding the world's belief systems may be acceptable from its limited perspective, but is not acceptable for the academy.[28] A naturalistic approach, he contends, is more objective and therefore ought to be the preferred method of study. Because a theological approach assumes a particular belief system it cannot be objective, he explains, and is, therefore, unacceptable for academic use. He challenges the popular notion "that the only proper approach to religions is 'from the inside,' and......argues that a clear distinction between a naturalistic approach—with its own explanatory apparatus—and religious approaches is necessary to achieve a coherent conception of what the study of religion is about."[29]

In Preus' judgment, a naturalistic explanation of non-naturalistic as well as supernatural belief systems is more fitting for the academy. He thus implicitly presupposes a definitive division in his explanation. That is, without explicitly defining religion, he reinforces the distinction as between the natural and the supernatural, thus affirming the dichotomy as well as implying that non-natural worldviews equal religion. He identifies a difference and makes the value judgment that a naturalistic method of inquiry is superior to any alternative. He implies that the religion category consists of whatever is incommensurate with his own naturalistic worldview.

Another champion of this perspective is Donald Wiebe. In his work, *The Politics of Religious Studies*, Wiebe strongly contends for the "need to reconsider the value of a return to evolutionary theory to re-establish a unifying framework for the study of religion."[30] It is his contention that "[a] study of religion directed toward spiritual liberation of the individual

---

28   Preus, *Explaining*, 205-211.

29   Preus, *Explaining*, xxi.

30   Donald Wiebe, *The Politics of Religious Studies* (New York: Palgrave, 1999) 292.

or of the human race as a whole, toward the moral welfare of the human race, or toward any ulterior end than that of knowledge itself, should not find a home in the university."[31] His assumption is that knowledge is gained only by the unifying framework of naturalism. Additionally, he quotes Maurice Cowling as offering the only acceptable action for scholars of religion, "as scholars, are committed, the only moral action to which they are commanded and the only 'social responsibility' to which their professional position compels them, is to use their energies in order to explain."[32]

But from what perspective ought the idea of religion be explained? He offers insight into his position when he suggests that a fruitful application of this particular framework of explanation can be found in Pascal Boyer's, *Religion Explained: The Evolutionary Origins of Religious Thought*.[33] The materialistic evolutionary method advocated here is considered by Boyer to be a productive way to explain the source and cause of religion. The reason for this, according to Boyer, is that the human mind has been prepared by a material process. Our minds, he says, "are prepared because natural selection gave us particular mental predispositions"—a predisposition for the idea of religion.[34]

This approach seems to be circular. The basic first principles of a naturalistic worldview are presupposed as the only acceptable methodology for explaining and interpreting the world's alternative belief systems. The worldview of naturalism is assumed to be true and is the lens through which all other perspectives are to be viewed and interpreted. Is this an objective approach?

Once again, an explanation that presupposes a definition of religion as the non-natural, or supernatural, and as something that arises is offered.

---

31   Wiebe, *Politics*, xiii.

32   Wiebe, *Politics*, xiv.

33   Pascal Boyer, *Religion Explained* (New York: Basic Books, 2001).

34   Boyer, *Religion Explained*, 3.

Both of these scholars propose a methodological naturalism for inquiry, interpretation, and explanation that is grounded in metaphysical naturalism. They each work within a prescribed worldview that allows them to interpret and explain those views that are contrary to their own.

How is this approach any more objective, what Preus demands, than a theological approach? With these examples it is apparent that explanation for Preus, Wiebe, and Boyer includes, indeed presupposes, interpretation, which includes a basic belief about ultimate reality, the meaning of experience, and the data of science.

These scholars argue that their own naturalistic worldview offers the best perspective for the proper interpretation and explanation of all other worldviews and therefore ought to be the preferred, privileged, position. The religion/science paradigm for them is valid. They argue that naturalism is fundamentally different than alternative views, it is 'outside' of all other belief systems, as opposed to adherents on the 'inside,' and is, therefore, in a better position to be more objective. They assume that their position is value-neutral. The interesting thing here is that they do not see themselves as working from within a position—a worldview. They view their assessments, their value judgments, as unbiased, neutral, and objective.

Theism, however, could make the same claim. For instance, naturalism and Hinduism are belief systems that need to be explained. Theists could claim that they can assess these worldviews, as well as others, as an 'outsider,' and would therefore be just as objective as a naturalist. Can naturalism explain itself as an 'outsider?' Obviously, no. The naturalist would then counter the theist with a charge of metaphysical bias because the theist has presupposed something about the ultimate nature of reality, thus making a biased judgment.

But has not the naturalist done the same thing? Methodological naturalism is promoted and defended as the only objective method of inquiry, while assuming metaphysical naturalism—a statement affirming the ultimate material nature of reality. The problem here, of course, is that naturalists want to claim neutrality, with no metaphysical bias, and, therefore, consider themselves more objective. They want to claim methodological naturalism only without recognizing their presupposed metaphysical foundation of naturalism.

A distinction has been made by Preus, Wiebe, Boyer and others and it appears to be based upon a natural/supernatural model. But this model, however, is inadequate. It does not take all views into account sufficiently. For instance, Buddhism, commonly believed to be a religion, does not fit into the category of naturalism or supernaturalism. For Buddhism, the 'real' world is of a non-material (spirit) nature and the spirit world is all that ultimately exists—the material world is illusory. The spirit world is all that exists and has always existed—it is eternal. This could be called spiritual monism. Conversely, material monism would be the view that all that exists is the material world and it has always existed (naturalism). Each view believes that all that exists is eternal, but differ on what it is that eternally exists—spirit or matter. The contradiction to both of these views, spiritual monism and material monism, is theism. Theism believes that some (not all) that exists is eternal and some is temporal (came into existence).

So, the worldview model being proposed in this project is based upon what is believed to exist eternally. That is, it is about the basic concept of existence and what ultimately exists. Epistemology and metaphysics are foundational. In other words, all worldviews believe either all is eternal or only some is eternal (some is not). This model more accurately categorizes the world's belief systems, which will be developed more in the final chapter.

The materialist metaphysical presuppositions of Freud, Preus, Wiebe, and Boyer, are quite clear. Just as it is demanded that the theist produce proof for its metaphysical presuppositions, so proof is required for the naturalist's metaphysical presuppositions. Naturalists need to prove rationally, that only the material world exists and that it has always existed, which has not been demonstrated.

This project, while it may be sympathetic to the concerns of Preus and Wiebe for wanting objectivity in scholarly inquiry, nonetheless, objects to their failure to recognize the presuppositions inherent in their own perspective. They not only implicitly define with their categories, but also determine the only acceptable method of inquiry. They argue that their own naturalistic worldview offers the best perspective for the proper interpretation and explanation of all other worldviews and therefore ought to be the preferred, privileged, position. They argue that naturalism is fundamentally different than alternative views, it is neutral and 'outside' of a particular category of beliefs, as opposed to 'inside,' and therefore in a position to be more objective.

But this simply is not the case and cannot be substantiated. They defend and promote methodological naturalism as the only objective method of inquiry because they assume metaphysical naturalism to be true—a significant bias. They offer no evidence or proof for metaphysical naturalism.

Nineteenth century theists attempting to explain views contrary to Christianity and labeling them 'alternative religions,' were doing something similar. Theists wanted to understand opposing views through the lens of Christianity whereas non-theists wanted, and continue to want, to understand opposing views through the lens of naturalism. Basic intellectual honesty is at stake here.

Why should naturalistic presuppositions be assumed to be the privileged interpreter of all worldviews? From a theist's perspective, could it not also be asked, from whence philosophical naturalism, why did it arise? It seems to make sense that the privileged view needs to be the proven, rationally justified, view.

A sound argument needs to be given in support of one approach over the other. Presuppositions need proof. It needs to be rationally demonstrated that naturalism is, if it is to be the privileged view, the only logical position to hold. Reasons must be given that produce a valid and sound argument. But as it will be demonstrated in more detail in chapter six, this cannot be done.

Wiebe laments that the science of religion has not yet found a place, its own identity, in the academy.[35] Could this be due to the fact that the idea of religion has not yet been clearly identified as an object of inquiry and research? The real question is, is it even possible? So far, it seems that no evidence can be produced that justifies two separate categories for the world's belief systems as they are currently conceived, or that naturalism ought to be the privileged worldview.

The subcategories of the worldview model can now be minimally understood as three groups; one which believes in a spirit reality only (Eastern views); a second group which affirms a spiritual as well as a material reality (Western theism); and a third group which affirms the existence of a material reality only (naturalism). In this light, the differences at the most basic level and the basis for the categories becomes more apparent.[36] But more explanation and clarity is still needed. Since these opposing views, as stated, are contradictory, only one can be rationally justified. Either a spirit reality is most ultimate and eternal, or a material reality is most ultimate and eternal.[37]

The real issue now becomes, can the worldview that affirms the existence of a spiritual, non-material, ultimate reality be rationally justified or can the worldview of naturalism rationally justify that only a material reality exists? Put differently, can one of these perspectives give reasons

---

35   Wiebe, *Politics*, 283-293.

36   These three categories of basic belief, spiritual monism, material monism, and theism along with a fourth, dualism, will be discussed further in chapter five.

37   This is to be understood as a contradiction when naturalism presupposes that all that exists is matter and eternal while theism presupposes that some spirit is eternal (creator) and at the same time some spirit and some matter (creation) is not eternal. When framed this way the 'all' that exists is eternal is in contradiction to only 'some' that exists is eternal. 'All' contradicts 'some.' Therefore one proposition must be true and the other must be false. There will be more discussion on this in chapter five. See Gangadean's, *Philosophical Foundation* for a more detailed exposition.

(rational proof) for its claim to knowledge and truth, or can they each only make dogmatic claims? The ultimate challenge then is for one view to produce rational proof that defeats all others. This is what naturalism has assumed it has done, but has it?

That the modern paradigm has been erroneously constructed should be coming into focus with the issue of knowledge still needing more discussion. When naturalism and the idea of religion are understood as just explained, the relevance of the question, why does the science and religion dialogue even matter, becomes more explicit. It is a matter of truth and error, and as Sam Harris has argued, life and death. Beliefs have consequences, personally and culturally.

2.5 Worldview Studies

If there is no basis for a 'religion' category and if no view has been rationally justified, then what is the role in the academy, if any, for what has come to be called 'religious studies?' With the popular paradigm dissolved and the idea of religion undefinable, it would allow scholarly inquiry from a much broader base. Religious studies could be termed 'worldview studies,' which would include naturalism as one particular worldview. Naturalism would be understood as an alternative worldview consisting of beliefs and practices just as Christianity or Buddhism. If preferred, each of these belief systems could also be termed ideologies. If the world's belief systems, including naturalism, are understood as beliefs that inform and shape the varied cultures of the world for the purpose of attaining meaning, then progress in understanding can be made. Worldviews have differences of belief at the basic level and will therefore influence cultural expression differently. What is believed to be ultimate reality will determine interpretation and explanation of existence and the experience of it. Naturalism will produce a different culture and set of values than, say, Taoism or Hinduism. The particular labels, for instance Christianity, would be retained as a general identification moniker.

University Religious Studies research programs could then be dedicated to the investigation of how worldviews function, interrelate, and influence cultures. Basic beliefs would be identified and the consequences of those beliefs could be traced through all the various academic disciplines. Researching and studying theories of religion, such as the classical theories, would be seen as irrelevant except as an outdated and inaccurate historical method.

Arizona State University is one research university that may be moving in this direction—at least it appears to be. In order to better facilitate the end just described, Arizona State University has recently merged the disciplines of Philosophy, History, and Religious Studies. Perhaps, with this move, it could be conceived that, in a broad theoretical sense, History and Religious Studies would gather and describe data, whereas Philosophy would categorize for rational consistency and interpretation beginning with basic belief. Arizona State University's Religious Studies program has recognized this point, to an extent, and addresses it on its university webpage. Generally speaking, this present project follows this pattern by merging disciplines. ASU's webpage states;

> For a long while many westerners have tended to think that religions are either "dying out" or have been relegated to the private sphere where they have little public or political importance. Recent events in the United States and around the world, however, have made it harder and harder to sustain this view. In our increasingly cosmopolitan world, the need to understand the root beliefs and values of diverse cultures has become a political and moral imperative. The academic study of religion seeks to explore the deep intersections between religions and cultures which have shaped, and continue to shape, personal and collective identity.[38]

---

38   https://shprs.clas.asu.edu/religious_studies. Jose Casanova addresses the issue of the de-privatization of religion in his book, *Public Religions in the Modern World* (Chicago: The University of Chicago Press, 1994).

The implication here is that it is the mission, a 'moral imperative,' for religious studies to interpret and explain the meaning and significance of the diverse beliefs and practices of the views in the category—religion. Understanding "root beliefs" is important. Root beliefs establish the basis for worldviews, or paradigms, in the Kuhnian sense, that shape what is acceptable cultural life. As Barbour has noted, "[a]s scientific models lead to theories by which observations are ordered, so religious models lead to beliefs by which experiences are ordered. Beliefs, like theories, can be propositionally stated and systematically articulated."[39] The idea here is, as stated above, that beliefs produce consequences. Beliefs (metaphysics/epistemology) determine behavior (ethics).

The category of religion, once considered by secularism to have been relegated to the area of personal piety—back to the beginnings of its original meaning—or on its way to extinction, now seems to be experiencing a type of renewal. Put differently, it was believed that naturalism would eventually preclude the existence of all other views. Not only does the Religious Studies department acknowledge the perseverance of these other views, but also deems it a moral obligation to know them. But whether dying out or resurging, the category remains the same—distinct from what is perceived as the privileged, more rational view of naturalism, or non-religion. Nonetheless, perhaps this is a move in the right direction, one that recognizes the idea that both secularism and religion are social constructs with no *sui generis* status.

Given this context, university research programs in religious studies then, at least at ASU it would seem, serve the role of descriptive sciences for the purpose of understanding anthropological and sociological interrelationships. Beliefs and practices of the various so-called religions (worldviews) are critically analyzed through the work of these research programs with the goal of understanding the implications for cultural life. The same

---

39   Barbour, *Myths, Models and Paradigms*, 119.

Arizona State University Religious Studies webpage says as much with its statement,

> Religious Studies brings together perspectives and approaches from history, sociology, anthropology, philosophy, and literature to gain a more comprehensive understanding of the individuals and traditions that constitute religions and cultures.

This statement appears to suggest a conception of religion that is more than personal views expressed in private. It intends to approach the study of so-called religion as an integral component of culture or even as fundamental belief systems that inform and shape culture. This approach is a departure from the former norm that conceived of religion as an add-on component expressed in personal belief and practice. Therefore, to study religion would encompass a broader cultural study rather than simply the study of private beliefs. When considered in this light, religious studies could also be conceived as worldview studies. Understood in this way, however, would mean leaving the popular view of religion behind, along with the category dichotomy.

With ASU's revised mission statement, the door is open to understand all of the world's belief systems, theism as well as naturalism, as worldviews that inform and shape civilizations and cultural life. As the statement above indicates, "[t]he academic study of religion seeks to explore the deep intersections between religions and cultures which have shaped, and continue to shape, personal and collective identity."[40] Could this statement not also apply to so-called non-religious views such as naturalism? Does not naturalism also shape personal and collective identity? Perhaps naturalism as a belief system or worldview should be included as an object of study within the Religious Studies program. After all, as discussed above, naturalism and so called religion are formally and structurally the same—they both interpret and explain the nature of reality.

---

40   https://shprs.clas.asu.edu/religious_studies.

Beliefs at the most basic level, the metaphysical level, whether theistic or naturalistic, determine behavior and practice. While the mission statement offers a modicum of hope for a more objective approach to understanding diverse worldviews, the prevailing paradigm is, nonetheless, still well-entrenched and in need of reformulation.

2.6 Summary

Though a theistic, or so-called religious, worldview dominated the West for well over a millennium, the past two centuries have produced continued decline for theism. This decline can be observed most significantly in the academy where the naturalistic view has ascended to supremacy. Naturalism, as one belief category, has been determined by modernity to be more rational, if not the only rational view, and, therefore, considered more authoritative and believable. As such, it is the privileged position. The idea of religion, on the other hand, is considered to be faith dependent and has not produced the proper evidence, or proof, to warrant any type of knowledge to substantiate truth claims suitable for dialogue in the public square.

Religion is grounded in belief, and science is grounded in knowledge, it is said. Therefore, it is assumed that a religious view essentially fails to pass the bar of rationality. Hence the dichotomy, reason and naturalism v. faith and religion, developed forming two separate categories of belief, each having its own interpretation and explanation regarding the nature of existence. The category of religion, and eventually world religions, then became the group of beliefs, or belief systems, that were outside of, and incompatible with, the rational, naturalistic perspective.

This understanding has become so much a part of and so entrenched in Western thought life that to imagine an alternative is almost unthinkable. The divide is often viewed in terms of binaries such as the holy and the profane, nature and grace, faith and reason, sacred and secular, or fact and value, to mention a few. Talal Asad has noted that these binaries "pervade modern secular discourse, especially in its polemical mode" and adds that they express that which is in opposition to the secular.[41] In light of this, questions such as, what is fundamental to the dichotomy and how is it justified, are paramount. Can any current approach to understanding the relationship between religion and science be substantiated apart from careful analysis of presuppositions? The prevailing mindset, or 'modern conceptual scheme,' needs to be critically analyzed, and most specifically, the idea that naturalism is more rational and therefore has grounds for being the privileged position.

The point here is that the academy is aligned with this view and assumes it to be objective and neutral. So-called religion generally, and Christian theism specifically, no longer has the esteemed position of sole interpreter and explainer of reality in the public square of Western culture that it once did. Rather, it has been relegated to the area of personal piety.

A naturalistic understanding of the world, particularly in the citadels of higher learning, has become dominant and has assumed the role once held by theism, thus marginalizing theism and determining it to be intellectually untenable and even irrelevant—hence, the assignment to the area of personal values only. Compared to the nineteenth century, theistic belief in the academy today and, indeed, belief in any transcendent reality, as Charles Taylor has argued, has been virtually vanquished. The idea of two mutually exclusive categories with the claim to knowledge as the dividing factor appears to be permanently fixed in the Western cognitive structure.

With what has been said so far, it is clear that Western modernity has been successful at shaping how its own idea of religion ought to be conceived. Modernity's development of science has defined religion to satisfy its purposes making the two categories unavoidably related and mutually exclusive. Modernity has divided the world's belief systems in such a way that favors a naturalistic worldview and is perceived as the rational view, against non-naturalistic worldviews that are perceived as non-rational.

---

41   Talal Asad, *Formations of the Secular* (Stanford, CA: Stanford University Press, 2003) 23.

The perceived rational view is the favored or privileged view and, therefore, the preferred view in the academy. Because of the divide, tension between the views has been the result. If the rational view is the privileged and preferred view, as it should be, then it is requisite for the view holding that position to demonstrate its rational coherence by its conformance to reason and meaningfulness. If it cannot, then it ought to be abandoned as the privileged position.

Theism lost this position and was replaced because it could not demonstrate its rational coherence, but rather embraced fideism—belief without proof. But can its replacement do any better? The answer to this question will continue to be explored in subsequent chapters.

As emphasized above, the modern understanding of religion and science cannot be isolated from the general and overall rise of modern Western thought. The making of religion and philosophical naturalism were a part of, and products of, this historical process. The philosophical precursors will now be explored in the next chapter.

But before moving ahead, a clarification is first in order. The assessment regarding the decline of theism and the rise of naturalism is not to suggest that religion, as commonly understood, is losing adherents or disappearing, but rather, that its intellectual currency in the academy has lost its value as a truth claim. But in spite of the loss and the rise of the naturalistic worldview, alternative belief systems (religions) are, nonetheless, still thriving and even expanding.[42] Other worldviews continue as viable options to the exclusive claims to knowledge made by naturalism. As a topic for another project, a valid question could be, why is this occurring?

---

42   See Philip Jenkins, *The Next Christendom: The Coming of Global Christianity* (New York: Oxford University Press, 2002). Also see Rodney Stark and Roger Finke, *The Churching of America, 1776-2005: Winners and Losers in Our Religious Economy* (New Brunswick, NJ: Rutgers University Press, 2005). These works show expansion of so-called religions in various parts of the world.

3

Philosophical Precursors to Modernity's Making of Religion

THERE WAS A time when the idea of religion, more specifically Ju-deo-Christian theism, and science were considered complementary. Theo-logians and the new 'scientists' viewed all truth as God's truth and were engaged in the mutual pursuit of the same end. But by the end of the nineteenth century this relative harmony experienced an unparalleled breech that prevails to the present. What were the causes of this breech? How did the idea of religion end up as a distinct category separated from scientific inquiry and often considered at odds with it?

The answers to these questions are in part due to an epistemologi-cal shift that took place in earlier centuries and subsequently paved the way for the nineteenth century growth of naturalism (the philosophical perspective of modernity) to move into a dominant worldview. The ques-tion of knowledge and how it was to be qualified as knowledge became the paramount question with which rising modernity would wrestle. This new worldview needed rational justification and that justification was to be found in its understanding of knowledge. From the eighteenth century Enlightenment forward, the view that believed that it possessed knowledge and could demonstrate it, would prevail as the true light for human culture and, therefore, qualify it to define reality.

The theistic worldview, through a series of epistemologically related intellectual revolutions, beginning most recently with the sixteenth century Protestant Reformation and extending through the early twentieth century, lost its exclusive position as the definer of reality for the Western world and was usurped by a naturalistic view. The claim to rational superiority by the new naturalistic view was resounding and appeared to be decisive. The following will explore some of the philosophical (epistemological) and theological precursors that made the transition from the pre-modern period to the modern possible, which was necessary for producing the categories of religion and science.

3.1 From Pre-modern to Modern

The decline of the Christian theistic worldview in the West took place progressively on several fronts. As the predominant view, theism experienced a significant threat to its sense of unity when the exclusive authority of the Roman Catholic Church was challenged. The crisis of authority precipitated by the Protestant Reformation made an absolutely radical break with the past seem mandatory.[1] Cultural upheavals in sixteenth century Europe severely eroded various concepts surrounding the prevailing theory of knowledge of the time—one rooted in authority.[2]

With the collapse of traditional authority structures, explains religion historian, Jeffrey Stout, disintegration of the terms closely connected with knowledge such as certainty, demonstration, opinion, probability,

---

1   Henning Graf Reventlow, *The Authority of the Bible and the Rise of the Modern World* (Philadelphia: Fortress Press, 1985) 3. From the Protestant Reformation, says Reventlow, also came a new understanding of the authority of the Bible.

2   Reventlow, *The Authority of the Bible.* Reventlow argues that biblical criticism and the departure from biblical authority precedes Cartesianism and goes deeper into the fabric of the history of Christian theology. A large-scale cultural movement throughout Europe must be set alongside the Reformation as the most powerful force in the formation of the modern world.

and authority led to an epistemological crisis to which various philosophers sought to respond. This loss cannot be overstated with respect to its impact on the new modern mindset. A method by which to reconstruct normative standards for right judgment and regulation was necessary after the unsettling theological tensions of this time.

One such philosopher was René Descartes (1596-1650) whose response was to avoid the terms associated in any way with 'authority' and reconstruct a foundation for knowledge based on demonstration and absolute certainty.[3] Stout views Descartes' quest for certainty as a "flight from authority" designed to release morals and politics from traditional Christian theism. A new starting point—one that would transcend the epistemic disparity of the situation and be independent of history—was the desired goal.[4] In rejecting authority, says Stout, "Descartes tried to make received opinion and conceptual inheritance inessential to thought."[5]

The philosophical climate of the seventeenth and eighteenth centuries with the major preoccupation with epistemological issues, unavoidably, had an impact on Christian theism and the development of the categories, religion and science. Issues concerning the certainty and starting point of knowledge, beliefs and their justification, and foundations for knowledge all came under critical analysis in the early modern era. The outcome was a distinctively modern cognitive structure for belief justification—commonly known as foundationalism.

With this particularly Cartesian approach to knowledge, the epistemological assumptions of pre-modern authority were called into question and the subsequent implications for Christian theism and science were monumental. The dogmatic canons of the pre-modern mindset were no longer acceptable for knowledge. The transition from a pre-modern epis-

---

3   Jeffrey Stout, *The Flight From Authority*, (Notre Dame: Notre Dame Press, 1981) 6; In this work Stout seeks to excavate the numerous historical factors surrounding the sixteenth century crisis of authority that led to the rise of modern thought.

4   Stout, *The Flight From Authority*, 67.

5   Stout, *The Flight From Authority*, 6.

temology grounded in the basic beliefs of a received tradition to a rational structure built upon a foundation of self-evident first principles was a radical move. But in light of the cultural crisis of the time this is just what Descartes proposed. So what is foundationalism and what is its significance for the categories of religion and science?

3.2 Epistemological Foundationalism

Foundationalism, explains philosopher, Nicholas Wolterstorff, is a characteristically Western phenomenon and essentially a theory of knowledge and rationality, that is, "a theory of what is rational for a given person to accept, to believe."[6] The fundamental issue underlying foundationalism is one of belief justification. Beliefs are based, or grounded, on something. Beliefs need to be justified and foundationalism is a system that justifies or warrants beliefs. It is one particular epistemic logic or structure designed to provide a support or 'ground' for beliefs which, by themselves, have no support. An appropriate metaphor here would be a building.

Foundational beliefs for epistemic foundationalists are considered to be directly held self-evident truths that form the foundation for the superstructure of knowledge and are not inferred from any other belief or proposition. They are one's most basic beliefs and constitute direct or immediate knowledge and are usually considered bestowed by intuition. Through intuition the knower grasps with certainty 'clear and distinct ideas' (Descartes), 'impressions' (John Locke, 1632-1704), or 'sensations' (Bertrand Russell, 1872-1970). These foundational propositions are then true by correspondence with states of affairs in the physical world (modern empiricism).

The foundation stops the otherwise infinite regress of reasons and inevitable skepticism. If beliefs are to be justified then the regress must

---

6   Nicholas Wolterstorff, "Introduction," in *Faith and Rationality*, eds. Alvin Plantinga and Nicholas Wolterstorff (Notre Dame, London: University of Notre Dame Press, 1983) 2. Wolterstorff also states that foundationalism has been formulated as a theory of knowledge and as a theory of authentic science (scientia, Wessenschaft) 2.

end in a foundation of beliefs that require no additional reasons for their justification. Philosopher, Robert Audi, states it simply, "foundationalists tend to hold that justification belongs to a belief, whether inferentially or directly, by virtue of its grounding in experience or reason."[7] Beliefs held inferentially are considered rational if they are logically consistent with a more basic belief. Inferred beliefs are ultimately supported by the most basic belief or set of beliefs.

What makes these beliefs rational is that the inferred beliefs provide adequate evidence for the more basic beliefs and the more basic beliefs provide adequate evidence for those inferred. This approach to knowledge is attractive due to the human need for certitude and meaning. "What lures and inspires the typical foundationalist," notes Wolterstorff "is the conviction that it is possible for us human beings to have direct insight into certain facts of reality—to have direct awareness."[8]

Not just any proposition, however, is considered basic and foundational. Only those propositions that meet certain criteria qualify. The history of foundationalism has been extensive—from Aristotle to the present—and has modified the included definitive tenets. Ancient and medieval foundationalists tended to hold that a proposition is basic if it is either self-evident (e.g. $2+2=4$) or evident to the senses. Modern foundationalists—Descartes, Locke, Leibniz, and others—tended to think of a basic belief as one that is either self-evident or incorrigible. An incorrigible belief is one of which a person is immediately and indisputably aware, such as a feeling of hunger. The consensus seems to be that these three categories constitute what has been termed *classical foundationalism*.[9]

---

7   Audi, *The Structure of Justification*, 149. This description is given in contrast to the alternative structure for epistemic justification, coherentism, which says that justification belongs to a belief by virtue of its coherence with one or more other beliefs.

8   Nicholas Wolterstorff, *John Lock and the Ethics of Belief* (Cambridge: Cambridge University Press, 1996) xi.

9   Alvin Plantinga, "Reason and Belief in God," in *Faith and Rationality*, eds. Alvin Plantinga and Nicholas Wolterstorff (Notre Dame, London: University of Notre Dame Press, 1983) 58-9.

Wolterstorff identifies the goal of the classical foundationalist as to secure a sense of certainty and to "form a body of theories from which all prejudice, bias, and unjustified conjecture have been eliminated."[10] This was to be achieved by constructing a theoretical structure of knowledge on a foundation of certitude. Historian, Peter Gay, makes the point that pre-Enlightenment antecedents concerning the certainty and starting point of knowledge, beliefs and their justification, and the foundations for knowledge, were the means to accomplish that end.[11]

It is this type of belief justification that has become the distinguishing feature of modernity and a principal Enlightenment ideal. The concept became the basis for autonomy in human critical reflection and was designed for determining universal standards that all humans could reasonably believe. Epistemologically, the transition from pre-Enlightenment to modernity finds its principal perpetrators in Descartes and John Locke, whom Audi identifies as the beginning of two great traditions regarding reason, its capacities and its modes of activity.[12]

With his interest in reason and his intention to depart from traditional authority, perhaps Descartes was more a product of his cultural history than he realized. Philosopher, Stephen Toulmin, has observed that European thinkers, particularly the French, have had a recurrent preoccupation with the idea of "starting again with a clean slate." Toulmin calls it "the myth of the clean slate."[13]

---

10   Nicholas Wolterstorff, *Reason Within the Bounds of Religion*, 2nd edition (Grand Rapids: Eerdmans Publishing Co. 1976) 28.

11   Peter Gay, *The Enlightenment: An Interpretation* (New York: Alfred A. Knopt, 1966) 17, Peter Gay says "It has been traditional to delimit the Enlightenment within a hundred-year span beginning with the English Revolution and ending with the French Revolution." This places the pre-Enlightenment era prior to 1689.

12   Robert Audi, *The Structure of Justification* (Cambridge: Cambridge University Press, 1993) 459.

13   Stephen Toulmin, *Cosmopolis: The Hidden Agenda of Modernity* (New York: The Free Press, 1990) 175.

The quest for certainty and the equation of rationality were import-ant for Descartes and the rationalists, but they were convinced that "the modern, rational way of dealing with problems is to sweep away the in-herited clutter of traditions, clean the slate and start again from scratch." This notion has played a significant part in the intellectual and political history of France with the most spectacular illustration being the French Revolution.[14] Undoubtedly, Descartes, in keeping with French tradition, was seeking a clean slate with his intuitive turn to the subject.

Audi understands Descartes' paradigm for rationality as intuition stressing the intellect's insight into truth, its deductive power, and its ac-tive character. From an internal starting point, he seeks to build a knowl-edge of the world based upon the foundational notion of clear and distinct perceptions. As the mind surveys the field of experience and clearly fixes itself on an object, it then elicits the will's natural assent to the manifest truth. Knowledge acquired from perception, then, is an intuition of the mind.[15] We will later see that it is at this point of intuitive principles that the postmodern philosophers will object. It is also at this point that chap-ter six will assess reason's capability for establishing a starting point that is rationally derived (a rationally derived presupposition).

Descartes' motivations for achieving certitude were essentially apol-ogetic in nature—an attempt to defend Christian theism particular-ly against skepticism. With his method of "universal doubt," he sought certainty through securing a foundation for knowledge that would lead to logically unchallenged first truths and thus fortify his position against skepticism. "Cartesian epistemology," according to Stout, "begins by em-bracing the challenge of radical skepticism as sufficiently cogent to call for serious attention."[16]

---

14   Toulmin, *Cosmopolis*, 175.

15   Audi, *The Structure of Justification*, 459.

16   Stout, *The Flight From Authority*, 26. Additionally, that Descartes was responding to skep-ticism was certainly the case, says Stout. However, Descartes was also responding to the epistemic disintegration of the categories established by the scholastics and their division

Descartes argues for the acceptance of the truth claims of Christian theism by those without faith with an appeal to natural reason "for they might suppose," he says, "that we were committing the fallacy that logicians call circular reasoning."[17] Faith, for Descartes, is useless to persuade those who do not believe. Reason alone provides appropriate means to bring one to accept either religion or a moral life. Knowledge based on certitude alone, not probability, is acceptable to discredit unbelief. Therefore, according to Descartes, all knowledge that is considered only probable is rejected as knowledge.

The inevitable question before Descartes was, what constituted certitude and by what method could it be obtained? His answer was universal mathematics. With mathematics he believed he had found the means to achieve an objective viewpoint and grasp certitude. With this affirmation, theologian, Trevor Hart, contends that Descartes, in effect, "drove a wedge between the categories of faith on the one hand and knowledge on the other."[18] Hart is undoubtedly correct for the history of modern Western theoretical thought followed Descartes' lead and accentuated the dichotomy, which continues in the religion/science divide.

John Locke took a different approach to certainty and knowledge. For Locke, knowledge of the external world arises not through the inferential assent from the internal to the external, but through the multitude of perceptions from the outside that reach the receptive mind within. The attentive subject receives perceptual knowledge as a normal product of

---

between "knowledge" and "opinion." *The Flight From Authority*, 39-40. The Protestant scholastics were actually engaged in the same battle with the Cartesians, but not over unbelief, rather over whether rationalism was the proper response to unbelief. See Richard Muller, *Post-Reformation Reformed Dogmatics, vol. 1* (Grand Rapids: Baker Book House, 1987) 241-49.

17   Descartes, *Discourse of Method and Meditations* (Indianapolis: The Library of Liberal Arts) 61

18   Trevor Hart, *Faith Thinking: The Dynamics of Christian Theology* (Downers Grove: InterVarsity Press, 1995) 31.

sensitivity to the causal powers of objects, rather than through an act of the will and the active pursuit of clear and distinct truth.[19] Whereas Descartes' epistemology tended to be actively influenced by the will and, therefore, took the form of a voluntaristic rationalism, Locke's was mainly naturalistic and involuntarist empiricism.[20] Though different in epistemic approach (rationalism versus empiricism) the common philosophical goal of an indubitable universal foundation for knowledge and certainty was fervently and judiciously pursued by both.[21] A foundational type cognitive structure was the result.

Theologian, Ron Thiemann, a student of the transition from the pre-modern to modern, views the move by Descartes and Locke as a monumental shift away from the biblical epistemology of the Protestant Reformers and their belief that knowledge is presupposed as the gift of God's grace, to an epistemology in need of an 'indubitable foundation' and 'demonstration.'[22] A key feature of the new foundationalist epistemology was that beliefs needed to be justified by argument appealing to convictions held independently of Christian scripture, or special revelation. With this turn was the introduction of non-biblical referents being appealed to for belief justification. For Thiemann, epistemology and modernity are causally linked. Epistemology is the transporting vehicle and identifying quality of modernity. By rejecting authority, he argues, Descartes was in need of a new basis for belief justification, a neutral uni-

---

19   Audi, *The Structure of Justification*, 460.

20   Audi, *The Structure of Justification*, 461.

21   Nicholas Wolterstorff argues that Descartes' foundationalism was far more restricted and traditional in its scope and designed specifically for *scientia*, whereas Locke's was meant for a broader application with evidentialist implications for religious belief. Locke's foundationalism, more than Descartes', has shaped the modern mind. *John Locke and the Ethics of Belief* (Cambridge: Cambridge University Press, 1996).

22   Ronald Thiemann, *Revelation and Theology, The Gospel as Narrated Promise* (Notre Dame: University of Notre Dame Press, 1985) 9-15. Thiemann argues in this work that the knowledge of God as understood by the Protestant Reformers is contrary to Cartesian epistemology.

versal, which became rational demonstration.[23] This is clearly in contrast
to the theologians of the Reformation who held that knowledge is given
by God and is believed as a basic conviction and background belief.[24]

Descartes and Locke were arguing that these 'background beliefs'
needed rational justification. The fideism of the Reformers, the mere affirmation of belief without rational demonstration, was no longer adequate.
With foundationalism, a basis for knowledge was now established that
was not dependent upon testimony and authority. Historically, this is a
significant epistemological shift and turn toward a broader application
and use of the term religion. What was not grounded in a foundation that
was rationally derived was not considered knowledge. This condition precluded claims to knowledge that were grounded in tradition or authority,
thus the beginning of a divide—religion and science.

3.3 The Rise of Modernity

What is called modernity is much more than simply what is current. Enlightened modernity, grounded in the wider epistemological phenomenon
of foundationalism, has clearly produced a way of viewing the world that
is in sharp contrast to the way it was viewed in the pre-modern period.
The former way of viewing the world was eclipsed and replaced with a
new one—the modern. Following the European Renaissance, Protestant

---

23 Thiemann, *Revelation and Theology*, 12,13. For a thorough study of the Protestant scholastics
and the rise of rationalism see Richard Muller, *Post-Reformation Reformed Dogmatics* (Grand
Rapids: Baker Academic, 2003).

24 Thiemann, *Revelation and Theology*, 11, In contrast to an epistemology of neutral rationalism and demonstration, Reformation theology believed that knowledge was a gift of God
and, particularly, knowledge of God functioned as a basic conviction or background belief.
Background beliefs, as axiomatic convictions assumed to be true, formed the basis of the
coherence of a whole framework of other beliefs. On p. 160 FN 7, Thiemann states that a
background belief is derived from various "holistic" treatments of the justification of beliefs.
Three of his several references are; Clark Glymour, *Theory and Evidence* (Princeton: Princeton University Press, 1980; W.V.O. Quine and J.S. Ullian, *The Web of Belief* (New York:
Random House, 1970); Nicholas Wolterstorff, *Reason Within the Bounds of Religion* (Grand
Rapids, MI: Eerdmanns, 1976).

Reformation, and the work of Descartes and Locke, the time was right for the dissolution of accepted institutional, authoritative, norms and a restructuring with contrasting individualism and subjectivism in view. The new cognitive structure, foundationalism, emerged as the predominant distinguishing feature of the shift from pre-modern to modern thinking. Modernity became definitively characterized by a foundational type knowledge theory inextricably linking the intellectual mindset and trends of the seventeenth century and the beginning of the modern era. The transition from pre-modern to modern occurs in the immediate post-Reformation, or pre-Enlightenment, period and it is in the pre-Enlightenment era that the rise of the modern cognitive structure has been identified.[25]

The changes expressed themselves in a *modern* outlook and to properly define modernity is not an easy task. The most famous attempt is arguably Immanuel Kant's. With Descartes as his philosophical father,[26] Kant characterized the whole Enlightenment age as the emergence of humanity from its self-imposed "indecision and lack of courage to use one's own mind without another's guidance." What this meant for Kant was freedom—"freedom to make public use of one's reason in all matters."[27] Endorsing Kant's view, Georg W. F. Hegel (1770-1831) followed with a similar statement when he said, "The greatness of our time rests in the fact that freedom, the peculiar possession of mind whereby it is at home with itself in itself, is recognized."[28] For Hegel, the principle of the modern era was the Protestant principle of autonomous individual thinking and its philosophical beginning was with Descartes.

---

25 See FN 11 above for dating the pre-Enlightenment era.

26 Toulmin notes that Kant's work did not come out of "blue sky," but was rooted in the rationality formulated by Descartes, *Cosmopolis*, 175.

27 Immanuel Kant, "What is Enlightenment," in *The Enlightenment*, ed. Peter Gay (New York: Simon and Schuster, 1973) 384-5.

28 G.W.F. Hegel, *Lectures on the History of Philosophy, vol. III* (New York: from Phil. disc., Habermas, 16) 423. Hegel believed that the principle of the modern era, the Protestant principle, was autonomous individual thinking and its philosophical beginning was with Descartes. 131-2.

Beginning with the premise that knowledge constructed on a self-evident foundation is autonomous, Kant and Hegel developed the idea that human beings had the capability to re-form their rational faculties within their ostensible limitations. With the shackles of tradition and authority of the Christian Church gone, an exhilarating sense of liberation emerged. Unrestrained by the strictures of medieval conventions and empowered by the individualism spawned during the Protestant Reformation, autonomous human reason was free to explore all the putative bastions of previous eras and view the future optimistically from a new perspective. Philosophy received a new stature. In Kant, says Toulmin, "the French Enlightenment's social ideals found philosophical expression."[29] Traditional ways of understanding the world and the organization of it, which had previously been determined by the medieval Church, were rejected in favor of ways that were believed to be better and more effective—and essentially, modern.

With the eclipse of traditional authority, those better ways were determined and guided by autonomous Reason, which became the guiding light for knowledge and truth for modern enlightened humanity. The idea here, as philosopher, Colin Brown, puts it, was "to strip Christianity of such extras as faith and belief in a supernatural God who personally intervenes in human affairs."[30] The result, says Brown, was "universal human reason as the supremely commanding principle and, hence, 'a fully attenuated Deism.'"[31]

For Kant, Hegel, and others, offering autonomous Reason as a viable alternative to traditional authority seemed most tenable. After all, Wolterstorff comments, it is an intrinsic faculty and not an external authority. It is common to all people and it belongs to the very essence of what it is

---

29   Toulmin, *Cosmopolis*, 8.

30   Colin Brown, *Philosophy and the Christian Faith* (London: Tyndale Press, 1969) 103.

31   Brown, *Philosophy and the Christian Faith*, 103.

to be human. To follow the voice of Reason is to follow one's own leading and is not submitting to anyone—true freedom.[32]

Theologian, William Placher, describes this period as a movement toward objective standards that are determined in isolation from the value and practices of the culture in which they are made and as a way to understand the reasonableness and meaning of assertions.[33] The shift in perspective was viewed by many in the West as a positive move away from an oppressive authoritative tradition grounded in the Bible as divine special revelation that had shaped the understanding of the world and the nature of ultimate reality until that time. It was during the seventeenth and eighteenth centuries that philosophers and theologians began to change their thinking about God, that is, their language about God and God's relation to the created world and human moral effects.[34] These thinkers, he argues,

> [G]rew more confident about human capacities—about their ability to understand God and God's role in the world and to contribute to human salvation—and narrowed their understanding of what counted as reasonable articulation of and argument for faith. That combination of a kind of confidence in human abilities and constricting definitions of acceptable reasoning led theology astray.[35]

Starting with the late seventeenth century and leading to the present, several philosophical and theological perspectives precipitated by the Cartesian/Lockean paradigm can be identified that influenced and shaped intellectual trends and the future of a theistic worldview. Rationalism,

32   Nicholas Wolterstorff, "Introduction" in *Faith and Rationality,* 5.

33   William Placher, *Unapologetic Theology* (Louisville: Westminster/John Knox Press, 1989) 74, 75.

34   William Placher, *Domestication of Transcendence* (Louisville: Westminster/John Knox Press, 1996) 2.

35   Placher, *Domestication,* 2-3.

empiricism, idealism, materialism, and ultimately philosophical naturalism, the fruit of the Enlightenment project and its ideals, all contributed
to the eventual fall of the prevailing authoritarian culture and ushered in
modernity and the movement toward what has come to be called a secular culture. This period is characterized by Enlightenment thought and
represents a progressive move toward a radical naturalism, one devoid of
divine intervention and relevance.

3.4 John Locke and Evidentialism

With pre-modern tradition no longer considered a reliable source for
modern knowledge and wisdom, the inescapable cultural agenda became
apparent. Essentially, it consisted of two basic questions to which Locke
addressed his epistemic efforts, 'how do we go about deciding what to believe?' and 'how do we conduct our understandings?'[36] Locke, of course,
did not realize it at the time, but what he was devising would shape and
direct not only Christian theism's defense strategies, but a scheme for
modern thought for the next three hundred years. Nicholas Wolterstorff's
penetrating analysis of Locke offers valuable insight into the early stages of
his knowledge theory. Locke's unique contribution to the growth of modern thought was, according to Wolterstorff, the introduction of an ethical
aspect to the pursuit of knowledge and belief.[37] Whereas Descartes established a new cognitive structure by revising the boundaries and ground
rules for proper epistemic analytical reflection, Locke added the governing
aspect of *oughtness,* the ethics of belief, for imperative participation and
culpability.

Locke, argues Wolterstorff, was the first to develop and defend the
thesis that we are all responsible for our beliefs, and that to do one's duty
with respect to one's beliefs one must listen to the voice of Reason rath-

---

36   John Locke, *An Essay Concerning Human Understanding* (Great Britain: Wordsworth Clas-
     sics, 1998)

37   Wolterstorff, *John Locke and the Ethics of Belief,* xiv.

er than that of tradition. Tradition, after all, says Locke, "is filled with error" and should not be considered the bar of truth for the elimination of falsehood.[38] In all things Reason was to be the guide. More so than Descartes, "Locke was the great genius behind our modern ways of thinking of rationality and responsibility in beliefs."[39] Locke's epistemology was his response to the cultural crisis of the day. He introduced to the modern Western world that belief, particularly religious belief, must first be rational and to be rational a belief must be supported by evidence. demands that Descartes had laid Wolterstorff has termed Locke's axiom the "evidentialist challenge."[40] What he did, in effect, "was take the classical foundationalist down for scientific belief and lay them down for rational belief in general."[41]

The problem, however, was that rationality needed to be defined and criteria for right belief established. If the goal was to be rational, then parameters for rational belief needed to be set. No area of belief was left exempt and unexamined. Given the historical context and the skeptical view regarding biblical dogma and authority, theism, particularly biblical theism, also needed to meet the rational (evidential) standard. With such a strong view of rationality and rational belief it was imperative that standards be set that would qualify the evidence.

Locke met the epistemological challenge for evidence with a proposal that would govern the belief forming faculty. His formulation consisted of three principles, which, applied in succession, would lead to certainty, or knowledge. When confronted with a proposition for belief one must first begin with satisfactory evidence. The principle of evidence requires the acquisition of "evidence for and against the proposition such that each item of evidence is something that one knows and such that the totality

---

38   Wolterstorff, *John Locke and the Ethics of Belief,* 226.

39   Wolterstorff, *John Locke and the Ethics of Belief,* xiv; Wolterstorff qualifies this assertion by also stating that Locke had forbears and cohorts in this line of thought.

40   Wolterstorff, "Can Belief in God be Rational?" 136.

41   Wolterstorff, "Introduction," in *Faith and Rationality,* 6.

of one's evidence is satisfactory."[42] Once satisfactory evidence is secured, that evidence determines the "probability" of the proposition, which is the second principle. The third principle then, the "principle of appraisal," "examines the (satisfactory) evidence one has collected so as to determine its evidential force, until one has 'perceived' what is the probability of the proposition on that evidence."[43]

The ultimate goal for Locke was to address the issue of proper, or rational, belief and determine a method of assurance that would counter the enthusiasts and the notion that "anything goes." What belief is one justified in having? Underlying Locke's theory was the idea of possession. The evidentialist challenge consisted in possessing the proper beliefs: "Some beliefs we ought not to have. Some we ought to *have*. Some we are permitted to *have*. Some we are permitted not to *have*."[44] Propositions with proper evidence call for obligatory belief, and beliefs without proper evidence call for obligatory dismissal.

Locke's view was persuasive enough to influence epistemology for the entire modern era down to the present day. The fruit of Locke's work is abundant and his disciples are plentiful. The now famous comment by W.K. Clifford "To sum up, it is wrong always, everywhere, and for anyone, to believe anything upon insufficient evidence" is a clear commitment to Locke's principles.[45] Bertrand Russell, the renowned twentieth century philosopher, was emphatic with his proclamation that there is not enough evidence to justify belief in God.[46] And Brand Blanchard in his Gifford Lecture series is unambiguous about the ethical character of belief when he comments, "everywhere and always belief has an ethical

---

42   Wolterstorff, *John Locke and the Ethics of Belief,* 67.

43   Wolterstorff, *John Locke and the Ethics of Belief,* 73.

44   Wolterstorff, "Can Belief in God Be Rational?" 143.

45   W.K. Clifford, "The Ethics of Belief," in *Lectures and Essays* (London: Macmillan, 1879) 345.

46   Bertrand Russell, "Why I am not a Christian," in *Why I Am Not A Christian* (New York: Simon & Schuster, 1957) 32.

aspect...There is such a thing as a general ethics of the intellect."[47] Thus, for Locke, the right kind of beliefs must be in place, those that can be justified in a particular way.

3.5 Toward the Natural

With its new found epistemic tools in hand, modernity was equipped to repair the disintegrating knowledge structure and construct a new methodology independent of the authority of tradition. Beliefs would now be tested by an objective standard. The breach between the new *scientia* and the old authority gradually became more apparent with key proponents emerging.

Historian, Peter Gay, has noted that though characteristic Enlightenment ideas existed long before, they achieved their revolutionary force only in the eighteenth century. The era had a history with overlapping closely associated generations of philosophes each drawing from the work of its predecessors. With the work of Newton and Locke at the foundation, Montesquieu and Voltaire represented the first group, Hume, Rousseau, and Diderot, the second, and Lessing, Kant, and Jefferson the third.[48] These were the dominant figures, but by no means an exhaustive accounting. It was the work of the second group, says Gay, "who fused the fashionable anticlericalism and scientific speculations of the first generation into a coherent modern view of the world."[49] Of these, Newton, Locke, Hume, and Kant are of particular interest here.

In addition to Descartes' *scientia* and Locke's concern for credible belief, the scientific work of Newton, a contemporary of Locke, and the empiricists posed major challenges for philosophy and theism. Scientific achievements were soon translated into a mechanistic and materialistic world view through literary works that captured the attention of the edu-

---

47   Brand Blanchard, *Reason and Belief* (London: George Allen & Unwin Ltd., 1974) 401.

48   Gay, *The Enlightenment*, 17.

49   Gay, *The Enlightenment*, 17.

cated public. With the impetus of enlightened modernity this new world view progressed to become the paradigm for all human knowledge. Scholarly disciplines had to be 'scientific' in order to be acceptable. Science defined what was reasonable and, therefore, true on the grounds of Lockean foundationalism.

With the work of Newton, Descartes, and Locke firmly in place, it did not take long until the basic tenets of traditional theism, particularly the doctrine of creation and the traditional authority of the Bible, were openly attacked. Any view not in compliance with the strictures of the new science was precluded from the category of what was reasonable. So-called religions, such as historic Christian theism, would only be acceptable if it met the standards of the natural. Foundationalism led thinkers to make a sharp distinction between "natural" religion—those beliefs that were thought to be demonstrable by reason—and 'revealed' religion—the beliefs and doctrines taught by the Bible and held by faith.

What soon evolved, following natural philosophy, was a form of natural theology, Deism, which supported the idea of universal beliefs determined by rational deduction and a common ground underlying various cultural and religious practices.[50] With natural theology, the rationalism of the Enlightenment found an acceptable alternative to biblical theism that would also satisfy the critical enlightened mind. By the end of the seventeenth century it was apparent that a shift in the relationship between revelation and reason was occurring.

Though Locke's epistemology was heavily directed by the power of natural reason, it still allowed for special divine revelation. Jeffrey Stout

---

50 Some, for example philosopher Colin Brown, have considered Deism to be a revival of Thomistic natural theology, *Philosophy and the Christian Faith* (London: Tyndale Press, 1969) 74, It needs to be noted here, however, that the natural theology of the medievals was quite different than what was being proposed by the Deists and Enlightenment thinkers. Nicholas Wolterstorff convincingly argues that "the medieval project of natural theology was profoundly different from the Enlightenment project of evidentialist apologetics." See "The Migration of the Theistic Arguments: From Natural Theology to Evidentialist Apologetics," in *Rationality, Religious Belief & Moral Commitment*, eds. Robert Audi, William Wainwright (Ithaca, London: Cornell University Press, 1986) 38.

points out that the Deists' even stronger emphasis on reason undermined Locke and granted reason a more significant role, such that only those tenets of traditional theology that could be established independent of special revelation ought to be accepted.[51] Thus, what was considered reasonable became the criterion and ultimate arbiter for acceptable theological belief. Rational demonstration was the only acceptable evidence for biblical credibility. Theologian, Hans Frei, anticipates the implications of this position when he comments, "[o]nce the Deist raised the question for external evidence for revelation the status of factuality for the meaning of revelation became a permanent item on the agenda of religious argument."[52] With Deism, the formidable place of a divine authoritative scripture became questionable and confidence in Locke's original program, which included a place for special revelation, was shaken.

Deists, considering themselves part of the Christian tradition, raised two key issues, according to Frei, that would fan the apologetic flame and be the precursor for greater changes to come. The first was whether the very idea of historical revelation was even intelligible. Why God would reveal himself to only a small faction of the human race seemed odd when truth and human happiness could be attained through rational reflection. The second issue questioned the likelihood of whether such a thing as special revelation had actually taken place. How well attested are the biblical accounts, especially the miracle claims, they contested? The naturalism of the 'scientific age' and the weight of David Hume's skepticism would eventually cast doubt on their reliability.[53]

Though natural theology was devised to support the Christian worldview, its general approach stirred loss of confidence in the idea of special revelation.[54] Locke's earlier work *The Reasonableness of Christianity,*

---

51 Stout, *Flight From Authority*, 117.

52 Hans Frei, *The Eclipse of Biblical Narrative* (New Haven: Yale University Press, 1974) 138.

53 Frei, *The Eclipse*, 52-53.

54 Deists were not anti-Christian or outright skeptics. Their intent was to divest the Christian religion of meaningless notions such as the 'mystery' of revelation. See Frei's, *Eclipse*, 117.

followed later by William Paley's (1743-1805) *Natural Theology*, were both attempts to establish the credibility of Christian theism to the Deists apart from special revelation, through appeal to demonstrable evidence and natural reason. Locke's work in particular argued that "a good deal of the content of revelation lies within the reach of our unaided natural faculties."[55] Paley, building on Locke's empiricism, proposed an argument justifying belief in God by appealing to the apparent evidence of design found in the universe. He, like every other English-speaking thinker of the era, displayed an implicit trust in empirical investigation to accurately mirror reality.

The work of the Deists fueled the evidentialist challenge—that rational beliefs must be justified by sufficient demonstrable evidence. But the most significant development was to come during the eighteenth century with philosophers David Hume and Immanuel Kant. The work of these two giants was another key factor that undermined the credibility of biblical theism. Their effect on theism and theology cannot be overstated. The defense of the credibility of the Bible against naturalism and the demand for evidence faced a radical new challenge. Following Hume and Kant, the apologetic methods of Paley, and others such as Blaise Pascal (1623-1662) and Joseph Butler (1692-1752) would no longer be intellectually acceptable.

3.6 No Access to the Transcendent

The Deists asked the question whether special revelation of God had actually taken place. Hume and Kant asked the more basic question, whether knowledge of God and a transcendent realm was even possible. Though different in approach, their conclusions were the same. And while not willing to deny the existence of God, their work, explicating their answer to the knowledge question, has left a legacy of skepticism down to the present day.

---

55   Wolterstorff, *John Locke and the Ethics of Belief*, 128.

Theologian, Ron Nash, critically assesses the impact of Hume and Kant on Christian theism in his work *The Word of God and the Mind of Man*. In it he speaks of the 'gap' caused by David Hume and the 'wall' created by Immanuel Kant, both metaphors indicating their effect on epistemology.[56] Hume's major threat to Christian theism, argues Nash, was not from the theories for which he gained notoriety, that is, his views on theistic arguments and miracles, but his undermining its claims to knowledge and objective truth. "Hume's gap is the rejection of the possibility of a rational knowledge of God and objective religious truth," thus continuing Descartes' effort of divorcing faith and knowledge.[57]

For Hume, beliefs are not determined by rational reflection, but rather, by instinct, habit, and custom. These experiences, which are essentially non-cognitive, lead us to believe in an external world. Reason has no power of persuasion toward a position of faith based on knowledge. Too much emphasis had been placed on reason, Hume argued, and philosophers had been entirely too optimistic when assessing its claims, thus also undermining Locke and the Deists.[58] Hume was clearing the ground, as it were, for the construction of a new edifice in the intellectual metropolis. His success in decimating empiricism stirred the architectonic intellect of Kant.

Not willing to accept Hume's skepticism, Kant, like Descartes earlier, set out to make room for knowledge. His system for acquiring knowledge places the human mind as the formulator of the external world. The mind is structured to categorize experience and this gives knowledge its form and structure. The altering effect of the mind has the unfortunate consequence of causing a radical disjunction between the world as it appears (and is known) and the world as it really is. Since the mind mediates and

---

56 Ronald Nash, *The Word of God and the Mind of Man: The Crisis of Revealed Truth in Contemporary Theology* (Phillipsburg, NJ: P&R Publishing, 1982) His primary goal with this work is to explore the extent to which the human mind can receive and understand divine revelation.

57 Nash, *The Word of God*, 22.

58 Nash, *The Word of God*, 17-24.

edits the sense data from the external world by its categories of under-standing, the real world (the *noumenal*) is never contacted. All that can be known is the *phenomenal* world, the world known by the senses. That which is in the noumenal realm (the metaphysical) is forever unattainable. Reason is restricted to the world of sense experience. Only the phenome-nal can be known and since God is by definition not a possible object of sense experience, but transcends the mind's categories, God, therefore, is unknowable.

Kant's system, says Nash, "had the effect of erecting a wall between the world as it appears to us and the world as it really is…Hume had his Gap: Kant had his Wall."[59] God, for Kant, is cognitively both unknown and unknowable.[60] If Christian theology was led astray by Enlightenment thought, then Kant applied the blindfold.

With his distinction between the noumenal, to which human access was denied, and the phenomenal, Kant believed he was making room for faith. Reason dealt with the facts of sense experience while engagement with God was not an item for factual consideration with respect to proof or disproof, but a matter of faith. Reason functioned within the realm of certainty, and faith with those things of an intuitive nature, thus further dividing any perceived compatibility between natural science and Chris-tian theology.[61] Kant's transcendental categories were so convincing for

---

59   Nash, *The Word of God*, 27.

60   The term "cognitive" here is meant as propositional knowledge as opposed to an awareness or feeling.

61   Historian, George Marsden, observes that Kant's distinction between the phenomenal and noumenal led to the restricted meaning of the term 'science' to mean only the physical sci-ences contrary to its etymological meaning of 'knowledge.' Kant's distinction also led to the eventual decline in metaphysics and ultimate relegation to the realm of 'mystery' and insus-ceptible to scientific inquiry. "The Collapse of American Evangelical Academia," in *Faith and Rationality*, eds. Alvin Plantinga and Nicholas Wolterstorff (Notre Dame, Ind.: Notre Dame Press, 1983) 245-6.

modern thought that they have been a virtual insurmountable obstacle for metaphysics to overcome.[62]

Critical of this bifurcation, theologian, Trevor Hart, accurately assesses its implications when he says, "This distinction effectively removed theology from the sphere in which rational discourse and argument is deemed appropriate."[63] Theologian, Gordon Kaufman, and his imaginative construction of God is a contemporary example of the effect of Kant's wall and a representative of Hart's point. For Kaufman, "God is mysterious and beyond all human knowing."[64] The only possible way of any reflection on the idea of God is through "the mind's supreme imaginative construct."[65] God is not known cognitively, but only through the non-rational faculty of the community imagination in history. In Kaufman's view, comments Hans Frei, it is the task of philosophical theology, through the academy, to adduce "the underlying criteria of meaningfulness and universality that would justify the deployment of this type of concept."[66] The two functions of the concept 'God,' for Kaufman, thus "are the relativizing and the humanizing of the world."[67]

Theologian, George Lindbeck, takes Hart's critique a step further by pinpointing the basic problem with Kant's epistemology. Kant, explains Lindbeck, paved the way for the experiential tradition in theology by his "demolishing the metaphysical and epistemological foundations of

---

62   The works of the "Vienna Circle" and logical positivism including A.J. Ayer and the early Ludwig Wittgenstein have been representatives of Kant's influence on the metaphysics of the twentieth century. See *The Revolution in Philosophy*, ed. Gilbert Ryle (New York: Macmillan, 1960).

63   Hart, *Faith Thinking* (Downers Grove: Inter Varsity Press,1995) 43.

64   Gordon Kaufman, *The Theological Imagination: Constructing the Concept of God* (Philadelphia: The Westminster Press, 1981) 35.

65   Kaufman, *The Theological Imagination*, 22.

66   Hans Frei, *Types of Christian Theology*, eds. George Hunsinger and William Placher (New Haven: Yale University Press, 1992) 28-9 Frei notes that Kaufman's type of philosophical theology "takes complete priority over Christian self-description within the religious community called the Church." 28.

67   Frei, *Types of Christian Theology*, 28.

the earlier regnant cognitive-propositional views."[68] Kant left no access to God. Lindbeck further argues that Kant left religion impoverished, and Friedrich Schleiermacher (1768-1834) filled the breach with what he called "the feeling of absolute dependence," but the new ideas would be given a variety of different names as the new tradition developed.[69]

3.7 An Alternative Theism

One of the new names for Christian theism associated with the effect of Kant and Schleiermacher is liberal Christianity. With rational access to the noumenal closed by Kant, Schleiermacher pursued a new avenue for Christian theism and apologetic expression. Reacting in part to the dogmatic emphasis of the day and to romanticism, Schleiermacher's focus on the idea of religion was as an anthropocentric activity of the emotions.[70] Religion, for Schleiermacher, was more than a reductionism of knowing (per German philosopher, Christian Wolff, Kant's predecessor) and doing (Kant's ethical emphasis).[71] The essence of religion, he argues, is "feeling" and "Christian doctrines are accounts of the Christian religious affections set forth in speech."[72]

Theologian, J.K.S. Reid, with Christian apologetics in mind, says that Schleiermacher "deflects theological thought into a new and uncharted channel."[73] Whether his later interpreters understood him correctly or not, he became identified in a practical way with religion as feeling as opposed to religion as doctrinal propositions.[74] With Schleiermacher,

---

68   Lindbeck, *The Nature of Doctrine* (Philadelphia: The Westminster Press, 1984) 20.

69   Lindbeck, *The Nature of Doctrine*, 21, Lindbeck has termed it "experiential-expressivism."

70   See Hans Frei's *Eclipse*, 282-306 for a discussion of Schleiermacher's hermeneutics.

71   Schleiermacher viewed theology more as Christian self-description than a philosophical endeavor. See Hans Frei, *Types of Christian Theology*, 34-8.

72   Friedrich Schleiermacher, *The Christian Faith* (title to para 15).

73   J.K.S. Reid, *Christian Apologetics* (London: Hodder and Stoughton, 1969) 208.

74   Nash, *The Word of God*, 31.

theism moved away from the pursuit of rational justification for theistic belief and embraced a subjective and intuitive awareness—a move into non-cognitivism.

Reflecting his theology, Schleiermacher's apologetic approach was to persuade religion's "cultured despisers" (the young romanticists and intellectuals of Germany) that true religion is a matter of universal human "feeling" and has little to do with dogma and even rational thought. He represented liberation from outmoded authoritarian dogmatics, favoring a truly modern form of Christian faith that appealed to the modern secular culture without conflicting with science.[75]

This was a type of fideism, where no rational defense of the worldview is offered, is supported with arbitrary intuitive principles. Schleiermacher's fideism, building on Kant, represented an overt move away from direct confrontation with modernity's intellectual advances in favor of a position not attempting a support with rational proof.

With the theological views of Schleiermacher, the center of Christian theism progressively moved away from a transcendent view of God and more toward an immanentism and a focus on the subject rather than an objective metaphysics. Though the eclipse of rationalism was pending, the movement toward a more consistent naturalistic philosophy and theology was on course. Schleiermacher's emphasis on human experience embodying the essence of divine revelation and manifestation propelled subjective theology to the more radical views of Ludwig Feuerbach (1804-1872).

Feuerbach, Hegel's student, inverted the view of his professor and maintained that the infinite is in reality a projection of the finite. As a result, he changed the deterministic idealism of Hegel to a humanistic materialism. What Feuerbach implemented for his 'theology,' Karl Marx adapted to history as a whole. Marx's materialism emphasized the naturalistic movement from being to becoming without Hegel's Absolute Spirit

---

75   Stanley Grenz and Roger Olson, *Twentieth Century Theology* (Downers Grove: Intervarsity Press, 1997) 42.

and placed man's temporal life at the center of the process.[76] The idealism of Hegel was turned upside down allowing the mind of God to become synonymous with the mind of humanity.

Humanity, for Feuerbach, was the central point of natural process. He proclaimed, "I, on the contrary while reducing theology to anthropology, exalt anthropology into theology."[77] The effect of this maneuver, in keeping with modern Enlightenment thinking and a progression towards naturalism, is a materialistic view of humanity. For Feuerbach, "Man has his highest being, his God, in himself; in his essential nature, his species."[78] Thus, with the undermining of biblical anthropology by naturalistic anthropology, naturalism achieved its goal of proclaiming divine intervention and even divine existence irrelevant and unnecessary. Feuerbach inverted the Creator/creature relationship and transformed theology into anthropology, making theology a mere projection. The divine attributes became idealizations of human aspirations and capacities. Thus, the next step, Friedrich Nietzsche's proclamation "[t]he most important of more recent events—that 'god is dead,' that the belief in the Christian God has become unworthy of belief—already begins to cast its first shadows over Europe," was a relatively simple move.[79]

With the preponderance of philosophical developments from the time of Locke, an epistemological consensus regarding the place of theistic beliefs that were once shared in the Western world rapidly deteriorated. In addition, the belief in metaphysics as a transcendent reality that governed the affairs of the world fell under serious criticism. The new philosophic knowledge inspired by Hume's skepticism, Kant's phenomenalism, Hegel's dialectic, as well as the subjectivism of the religion theorists, Schleiermacher, and Feuerbach, called into question the truth claims of a variety

---

76   Gordon H. Clark, *Thales to Dewey* (The Trinity Foundation, 1997) 474-5.

77   Ludwig Feuerbach, *The Essence of Christianity* (Buffalo: Prometheus Books,1989) xviii.

78   Feuerbach, *The Essence of Christianity*, 281.

79   *The Complete Works of Friedrich Nietzsche*, ed. Oscar Levy, Vol. 9, *The Joyful Wisdom* (Edinburgh: T.N. Foulis, 1911) 275.

of Christian theistic beliefs. The creation of mankind and the world, belief in miracles, the literal reading of the Bible as the authoritative word of God, the hope of life after death with rewards and punishments, heaven and hell, conscience as the inner voice of God, the sacrificial death and resurrection of Jesus Christ, were replaced with a naturalistic explanation. In brief, beliefs that had not been questioned for centuries were now under the scrutiny of higher criticism and the enlightened intellect of modernity.

So predominant in the history of Western thought is the work of Hume and Kant that philosopher/theologian, Nancey Murphy, has convincingly argued that in the wake of Hume's skepticism two major philosophical and theological trajectories emerged that further impacted epistemological developments. In reaction to Hume, two separate traditions developed following either Kant or Scottish philosopher, Thomas Reid (1710-1796). From Kant's reaction came Schleiermacher and the Christian liberal tradition that followed. From Reid, a contemporary of Hume and Kant, came Old Princeton theology and the American conservative evangelical tradition.[80] Reid, building on Joseph Butler (1692-1752) and the early thought of William Paley (1743-1805), challenged Hume's skepticism with his 'Common Sense Realism.' Wolterstorff notes that Reid viewed Hume as continuing the crisis of faith and action caused by Descartes' proposed solution to the crisis he had identified. He was readily aware that Descartes introduced the 'way of ideas' and Locke and Hume followed them.[81]

---

80   Nancey Murphy, *Beyond Liberalism and Fundamentalism: How modern and Postmodern Philosophy Set the Theological Agenda* (Valley Forge, PA: Trinity Press International, 1996) 4-7, In this work Murphy argues that liberalism and fundamentalism have developed in parallel to each other. Also see Murphy's *Anglo-American Postmodernity: Philosophical Perspectives on Science, Religion, and Ethics* (Valley Forge, PA: (Boulder, Co.: Westview Press, 1997) 113-14, 87-112.

81   Nicholas Wolterstorff, "Thomas Reid on Rationality," in *Rationality in the Calvinian Tradition*, eds. Hart, Vanderhoeven, Wolterstorff (Boston: University of America Press, Inc., 1983) 44.

Kant's idealism and Reid's realism, being diametrically opposed, forced a division.[82] This split, explains Murphy, has been exacerbated by the philosophical developments of modern thought and is primarily responsible for the present divisions in Protestant Christianity.[83] Each approach sought to develop and appropriate their own unique theological agendas. Liberal theology constructed a view of the immanence of God and revelation, "not as an intrusion, but as a correlative to human discovery and God disclosing himself through human means and processes."[84] Conservatives built their understanding on belief in the intervening work of God through special revelation, which conveys authoritative information about human and divine realities. It is the Bible and not experience that functions, for conservatives, as the data for theology.[85] Both reject any kind of natural theology, that is, the use of Reason to gain knowledge of God.

With the redirection in theology, prompted by Hume, Kant, and Schleiermacher, came a different method for appropriating the Christian worldview. Christian liberalism, following Schleiermacher's lead, addressed the cultural application of Christian theism through a reconstruction of the Christian worldview accommodating it to a growing secularism. Liberalism's theological, as well as apologetic, method was designed around the experience of 'the believing subject' as the ultimate criterion and subject matter for theology.

Conservatives on the other hand, standing with traditional orthodoxy, rejected this approach in favor of objective authoritative propositions about God and the world as the ultimate criterion for theology. Both liberal and conservative theologies, Murphy contends, have shared the assumptions of modernity. Neither strategy was able to avoid the powerful

82 For more critical interpretation of Reid's realism see Nicholas Wolterstorff, *Thomas Reid And The Story Of Epistemology* (Cambridge: Cambridge University Press, 2001).

83 Murphy, *Anglo-American Postmodernity*, 87.

84 Murphy, *Anglo-American Postmodernity*, 88.

85 Murphy, *Anglo-American Postmodernity*, 88.

influence of modernity and epistemological foundationalism. The image of a structure with an immovable foundation was too appealing. They have both constructed their theologies on a theory of knowledge that justifies belief to a foundation.[86] Chapters 5 and 6 will critically analyze the need for a foundation for knowledge.

The distinction between liberal and conservative theology has essentially been their respective choice of foundations—universal experience for liberals and Scripture for conservatives. Murphy appeals to Old Princeton theologians, Charles Hodge (1797-1878), A.A. Hodge (1823-1886), as well as A.H. Strong (1836-1921), all greatly influential in the American evangelical movement, for support of her view.

On the liberal side, Schleiermacher is her selection pointing to his use of the 'awareness of absolute dependence,' common to all religions and available in principle to all people, as his foundational experience. She contends that an attempt to show that the Christian Bible "is in fact the expected revelation…Conservative apologetics from Locke's day to the present have attempted to shore up the basement…for a *foundationalist* use of Scripture."[87] Instead of a universal that is derived from experience, the conservative approach placed an inerrant and infallible Bible as the epistemic foundation. Both of these foundations, however, were fideistic (no rational justification) and would prove to be inadequate in the face of Kantian metaphysics.

Murphy's conclusions affirm that both liberal and conservative theologies and apologetic methods appropriated the assumptions of modernity.[88] She has also concluded that these appropriations by Christianity, constructed on the foundationalism of modernity, has been ineffective in its challenge of naturalism. What still needs to be addressed is whether the foundationalism established by modernity is a tenable epistemology. The

---

86 Murphy, *Anglo-American Postmodernity*, 89.

87 Murphy, *Anglo-American Postmodernity*, 90.

88 Murphy, *Anglo-American Postmodernity*, 90-97.

next chapter will illustrate how naturalism usurped the role of guiding light to the nations once held by theism.

3.8 Summary

The progression delineated above shows some of the critical philosophical developments related to modernity's making of religion. It begins in the world of the early seventeenth century with Descartes' 'flight from authority' and ends in the mid-nineteenth century with Feuerbach's 'deified humanity' culminating in the marginalization of Christian theism and the birth of a new naturalistic view of the world.

During this period, biblical authority as well as natural theology are supplanted by a new sense of the proper use of reason and the confident optimism of Baconian science reaching fruition. Enlightenment ideals, and specifically epistemic foundationalism as a key distinctive of modernity, have been identified and explored. Certainty was now believed to be found in universal norms or standards for truth, which could be determined either empirically (Locke), with uninterpreted sensations, or rationally (Descartes), with logically unchallengeable, self-evident first truths, and accessible by all rational thinkers. The idea of special revelation, scripture from God, was considered superfluous.

The Enlightenment dream of a universal standard of rationality that serves as a single method for determining what is true and what is false, and universally acceptable common ground for conversation is an Enlightenment ideal of modernity. This ideal was rooted in epistemic foundationalism that was ushered in and offered as the segue for a naturalistic view of culture and the universe.

4

The Modern Decline
of Christian Theism and the
Rise of Naturalism

WITH THE PHILOSOPHICAL precursors having already paved the way, one of the greatest oppositions to Christian theism and the idea of religion in general in the latter part of the nineteenth century came from the philosophical outlook that emerged from the natural sciences. The naturalistic view of the world, as outlined in the previous chapters, defined and informed the on-going philosophical and theological debate that has extended into the twentieth-first century. Whether explicit or assumed, a theory of knowledge was employed by modern philosophers of naturalism as well as by their critics. Epistemological foundationalism and its requirement for empirical evidence continued to function as the exclusive theory of knowledge for modernity as well as for all challenges to modernity's steady movement toward a naturalistic view during this period.

Conservative Western theologians, claiming to place their belief in the ultimate authority of the Bible and disdaining any type of natural theology, were no less immersed in the subtleties of the prevailing evidentialist belief structure of the era. Natural science, promoting itself as neutral with respect to metaphysics, was not, however, exempt from also employing the same theory of knowledge to achieve its desired ends. The Cartesian/Lockean epistemology of modernity served natural science's purposes well. Additionally, the emerging secular ethos, constructed on a foundation of natural science, had shaped the cultural consciousness, including conservative theology, by solidifying a common monolithic epistemology for analytical inquiry and reflection.[1]

By this time, the self-evident outlook of the once dominant theistic view had been severely challenged and forced into a defensive position. While Christian theism was not yet a minority view, it nonetheless, could no longer be assumed as the normative view. Theism's arguments from miracles and prophecies, the wisdom of God in creation, and the analogy between nature and Scripture continued to be employed. But these arguments, predicated on the ostensible evidence for an intelligent designer or an appeal to 'common facts' of experience as theistic proof, were no longer convincing.

---

1   According to Stow Persons, the end of the nineteenth century in America has been depicted as a time when the religious community was "at bay before a secular culture with which it was unwilling or unable to come to grips." To a large extent, he further states, this can be attributed to three ideological currents that were merging to form the intellectual matrix of the modern age. The Protestant Reformed tradition was the oldest, the democratic social ideology that had become firmly fixed in the American ethos during the nineteenth century was the second, and the most recent was the strong current of naturalistic ideas—a kind of popularized scientific philosophy arising out of positivism and evolutionary theory. These three streams formed a synthesis producing modernity as a worldview. Essentially, Enlightenment ideals found their way into the mainstream of modern life. Stow Persons, "Religion and Modernity," in *The Shaping of American Religion*, eds. James Ward Smith and A Leland Jamison (Princeton: Princeton University Press, 1961) 369-70. For this assessment Persons cites, Arthur M. Schlesinger, "A Critical Period in American Religion, 1875-1900," *Proceedings of the Massachusetts Historical Society*, 64, June, 1932, pp.523-547; Henry F. May, *Protestant Churches and Industrial America*, N.Y., 1949, 91-111; Thomas T. McAvoy, *The Great Crisis in American Catholic History*, 1895-1900, Chicago, 1957.

4.1 The Maturation of Naturalism

Naturalism emerged as a plausible alternative interpretive scheme—one based on the Baconian scientific method—and ultimately presented itself as the exclusive view of modernity. Facing the challenge, traditional theistic defensive strategies proved themselves deficient and inadequate to overcome the momentum of the new science and the inevitable naturalistic outlook. The overwhelming strength of this movement initiated a radical reassessment of the viability of those strategies.

As mentioned above, while the relationship between science and theism has been a debated topic for at least the past two centuries, several views have prevailed depicting the two as mortal enemies, friendly allies, or somewhere in between. But if a poll were taken today, the average person both inside and outside of academia would, most likely, side with those who sense a tension. Militaristic adjectives such as conflict, warfare, battle, and weapons have been common terminology in writings describing the relationship. Given that each affirms a different conception of ultimate reality, it would be hard to view in any other way.

Two of the most famous past promoters of the conflict, John W. Draper (1811-1882) and Andrew Dickson White (1832-1918), tended to magnify the tension that did exist, nurturing at least the perception of warfare. Draper, son of a Methodist minister and member of the science faculty of New York University, stated that "[t]he ecclesiastic must learn to keep himself within the domain he has chosen" and that "[r]eligion must relinquish that imperious, that domineering position which she has so long maintained against Science."[2] Draper's scathing sentiment was principally directed at the Roman Catholic Church for its repressive treatment of scientific achievement, though it was intended for Protestants as well.

---

2   John W. Draper, *History of the Conflict between Religion and Science* (New York: D. Appleton & Co., 1874) 367.

White, professor of history at Cornell, echoed Draper's attitude and was no less adversarial with his assessment. In his *A History of the Warfare of Science with Theology in Christendom* he wrote the following,

More and more I saw that it was the conflict between two epochs in the evolution in human thought—the theological and the scientific....an evolution, indeed, in which the warfare of theology against science has been one of the most active and powerful agents.[3]

Since this project is about the rise of philosophical naturalism and the marginalization of theism and, therefore, *prima facie* confrontational, the attention here will be directed at the conflict between the two.

If understood from the conservative Christian apologist's perspective, it is hard to conceive of the relationship at the end of the nineteenth century as anything other than one of conflict. Of course, even that proposition is predicated on how science is defined and understood as well. Though some scientists and even historians (e.g. White) objected to a 'religious' view having any influence on the natural sciences, the objective here will be to explore why many conservative Christian theists came to view science, at least the variety that was propounded during the last half of the nineteenth century, as a threat and how they responded. It is worth noting, however, that not all conservative theologians were opposed to the naturalistic theory of evolution in total. For example, Benjamin Warfield (1851-1921) and Augustus Strong (1836-1921), both Americans, and James Orr (1844-1913), a Scotsman, all eminent Protestant theologians, saw nothing problematic with the theory and adopted some version of it.

Whereas the eighteenth century proclaimed freedom from ecclesiastical authority in the name of enlightened reason, the nineteenth century produced a viable system for interpreting experience and the world

3   Andrew D. White, *History of the Warfare of Science with Theology in Christendom* (Albany, OR: Ages Software, [1896] 1997) 12, 14.

apart from any kind of theism or divine revelation and, thus, marginalized Christian theism even further within the trend toward modern secularization. Clearly, the tendency of modernity was to distance itself from divine necessity. The theistic hypothesis, proclaimed Pierre Simon Laplace (1749-1827), was indeed no longer needed. Laplace helped substantiate this position with his nebular hypothesis for the origin of the universe, which precluded God as the necessary first cause.[4]

This new developing tradition, or secular view of the world, was permeated with optimism. John Draper enthusiastically expounds on the virtues of the new perspective with these comments,

> The ecclesiastical spirit no longer inspires the policy of the world...The intellectual night which settled on Europe, in consequence of that great neglect of duty, is passing away; we live in the daybreak of better things. Society is anxiously expecting light, to see in what direction it is drifting. It plainly discerns that the track along which the voyage of civilization has thus far been made, has been left; and that a new departure, on an unknown sea, has been taken.[5]

Draper's attitude was not unique but was representative of much of the academic mentality. Christian theism rapidly lost its position of authority concerning creation, the nature of mankind, and the doctrine of sin and was beginning to feel the undercurrents stemming from the new developments in the academy.

The line drawn by Descartes and Locke between faith and reason now also extended to natural science and specifically Christian theism. Effectively, it was faith and theology relegated to one domain, as Draper had demanded, and reason and science to another. The result of this move, says Frederick Gregory, "was to redefine the domain and prerogatives of

---

4   Roger Hahn, "Laplace and the Mechanistic Universe," in *God and Nature*, 256.

5   Draper, *History of the Conflict*, v-viii.

religion in such a way that scientific explanations did not clash with religious expression."[6] With this understanding, gaining knowledge of the physical world was perceived to be an objective endeavor and did not involve a religious dimension.[7] The product of scientific investigation was believed to be value neutral 'brute facts' and its success perpetuated the faith/knowledge dichotomy reminiscent of Kant's 'wall.' Undoubtedly, the fruition of this development led to Martin Marty's observation that secularization took place through a peaceful separation of 'religious areas' from the secular and scientific. The harmonious coexistence continued as long as true science was always the base of proof for true religion.[8]

Moreover, theology, pressed by concerns of relevancy stemming from the influence of Protestant scholasticism and the positive move by the new science, offered an accommodating alternative with the work of Schleiermacher. While the theological ingenuity of Schleiermacher refused to be bound by a doctrinaire concept of nature, his insight was both poignant and prophetic when he wrote,

The further elaboration of the doctrine of creation in dogmatics comes down to us from times when material even for natural science was taken from the Scriptures and when the elements of all higher knowledge lay hidden in theology. Hence the complete separation of these two involves our handing over this subject to natural science, which, carrying its researches backward into time, may lead us back to the forces and masses that formed the world, or even further still.[9]

---

6   Frederick Gregory, "The Impact of Darwinian Evolution on Protestant Theology," in *God and Nature*, 385-6.

7   Gregory, "The Impact," 386.

8   Martin Marty, *The Modern Schism: Three Paths to the Secular* (New York: Harper & Row, 1969) 98.

9   Friedrich Schleiermacher, *The Christian Faith*, Vol. 1 (New York: Harper & Row Publishers,1963) 150; cf. *On the "Glaubenslehre": Two Letters to Dr. Lucke*, trans. J. Duke and F. Fiorenza (Chico, CA: Scholars Press, 1981).

By this statement Schleiermacher affirms an authoritative position for natural science in theological inquiry concerning origins and the nature of humanity. That special revelation is the exclusive source for knowledge of origins was eclipsed by the growing belief in the autonomy of scientific investigation as the only valid interpreter of the world and not the Bible or any other so-called religious text. Scientific historical criticism became the normative mode of inquiry for religious knowledge. The higher critics implemented a type of empirical investigation to evaluate the credibility and trustworthiness of the biblical documents, which oftentimes conflicted with traditional Christian beliefs. The dichotomy was being strengthened; the naturalistic view built on neutral brute facts in one category and contrary views would fall into the category of religion.

In an attempt to "penetrate behind the concrete issues…to the underlying problems which exercised the major parties in the debates," historian, John Dillenberger, has identified at least two achievements implicit in the new science that initiated the eclipse.[10] The first, says Dillenberger, is that "[a]ll aspects of faith or of revelation had finally to be as clear or as self-evident as the order of nature." It was this widely held assumption which gradually led to the demise of revelation as understood in its traditional form. Conservative theology failed to see the implications and did not rethink the concept of revelation, but merely continued their traditional methodologies for defending the credibility and veracity of the Bible.[11] The second achievement, Dillenberger argues, was that the new science had in fact become a philosophy and he explains the effect in this way;

The achievement of the movement was that of bringing the ideas associated with the new science into a coherent world view and of popularizing the results. Its task was that of organization and

10   John Dillenberger, *Protestant Thought And Natural Science: A Historical Interpretation* (London: Collins Clear- type Press, 1960) 13.

11   Dillenberger, *Protestant Thought And Natural Science*, 164.

of interpretation. The new ideas were brought into the orbit of a
shared culture, and thereby indirectly into the orbit of the common man.[12]

Science, as Schleiermacher had surmised, replaced scripture's once exclusive right to the interpretation of nature. A clear methodological principle
for understanding revelation (in nature) had emerged with a philosophical
direction to delineate the content of that revelation. As a result, an entirely
new tradition of reason and nature became a substitute for what was once
considered the exclusive domain of special revelation.[13]

But just exactly how objective is the inquiry of natural science was
the question that some began to ask. The position of neutrality by the
naturalists was a thinly veiled cover-up—a misunderstanding of the true
nature of science, it was argued. Though they are often unrecognized,
states British scientist C.A. Coulson, moral convictions are an integral aspect of the project of science. In his *Science and Christian Belief*, Coulson
comments that "science itself must be a religious activity."[14] Scientists are
God's heralds employed in the task of exposing God's revelation of himself in nature and thus avoid "an unbearable dichotomy of experience."[15]
When science is properly understood the fact that it is constructed on inherent religious presuppositions (a metaphysical scheme) becomes readily
apparent. The legacy of science betraying its religious convictions include
three assumptions; a search for common truth, the unexamined belief that
facts are correlatable and cohere in a scheme, and a belief in the order and
constancy in nature. For Coulson, these assumptions are enough to carry
science into the realm of metaphysics.[16]

---

12   Dillenberger, *Protestant Thought And Natural Science*, 133.

13   Dillenberger, *Protestant Thought And Natural Science*, 187.

14   Charles A. Coulson, *Science and Christian Belief* (Chapel Hill, NC: The University of North
     Carolina Press, 1955) 57, 30.

15   Coulson, *Science*, 31.

16   Coulson, *Science*, 57.

Dillenberger and Coulson were precursors, of sorts, to Thomas S. Kuhn and his monumental work, *The Structure of Scientific Revolutions*. In his work Kuhn recognized and developed the theory-laden nature of natural science. Phenomena are typically defined and interpreted in different ways depending on core beliefs and perspective. Phenomena, says Kuhn, are interpreted by "some implicit body of intertwined theoretical and methodological belief that permits selection, evaluation, and criticism."[17] The interpretive enterprise presupposes and articulates a paradigm, and the operations and measurements of scientists are paradigm determined.[18] Thus, the notion of value neutral science so ardently held by the Western epistemological tradition has been shown to be highly debatable, since the work of science is in fact predicated upon presuppositions, or core beliefs, regarding the nature of reality. Kuhn, following the philosophical thought of the early twentieth century, will be discussed more in the next chapter. How this understanding came about, and the related theistic apologetics, will be discussed in the following.

While theism was losing its exclusive position in the Western world through the nineteenth century, American Christian conservatives, still wanting to hold to Locke's vision, had until this time continued to view the Bible as authoritative for science and history in spite of the growing move toward naturalistic explanations. The Bible, for them, still had the authority to speak to science as well as to areas that science could not address. But what they did not quite understand was that the intellectual revolution in nineteenth century America, which resulted in scientific positivism, pragmatism, and historicism, also provided explanations that fit many social trends toward secularization. Whether Christian conservatives were willing to accept it or not, the strength of the movement toward naturalism and modern secularization was against them.

---

17   Thomas S. Kuhn, *The Structure of Scientific Revolutions*, Second ed. (Chicago: The University of Chicago Press, 1970) 17.

18   Kuhn, *The Structure*, 126.

In spite of the incriminating speculative geologies of Charles Lyell (1797-1875) and James Hutton (1726-1797), science and biblical theism were relatively compatible until the scientific revolution associated with biologist, Charles Darwin (1809-1882). An alternate explanation for the apparent order and purpose in reality, other than the cosmological argument from design, was now available. The raw data acquired from empirical investigation, the naturalists argued, could be understood best in terms of mechanistic natural forces. Explanations of a 'plan of creation' or 'unity of design,' according to Darwin, provided no actual information but merely served to hide ignorance.[19] Darwin's intention was to promote a positivist epistemology that limited science to mechanistic explanations. His rejection of special creation, explains Neal Gillespie, "was part of the transformation of biology into a positive science, one committed to thoroughly naturalistic explanations based on material causes and the uniformity of nature."[20]

The Bible, as well as theism in general, was no longer viewed as a necessary component for accurate assessment in the phenomenal realm and, therefore, what was believed to be neutral, scientific methodology, with the help of talented exponents, Ernst Haeckel (1834-1919) and Thomas H. Huxley (1825-95), turned its forces directly against Christian theistic thought.[21] The learner, says popularizer Huxley, needs to "seek for truth not among words but among things."[22] "Moreover this scientific 'criticism of life,' appeals not to authority, nor to what anybody may have

19   Nancy R. Pearcey and Charles B. Thaxton, *The Soul of Science: Christian Faith and Natural Philosophy* (Wheaton: Crossway Books, 1994) 116

20   Neal Gillespie, *Charles Darwin and the Problem of Creation* (Chicago: University of Chicago Press, 1979) 19.

21   George Marsden notes that "Only strongly institutionalized authority, as in the citadels of Roman Catholicism, was able to withstand such tendencies on a large scale, and then at the cost of sacrificing some academic respectability. "The Collapse of American Evangelical Academia," in *Faith and Rationality*, eds. Alvin Plantinga and Nicholas Wolterstorff (Notre Dame, Ind.: University of Notre Dame Press, 1983) 220

22   Thomas H. Huxley, "Science and Culture", *The Norton Anthology of English Literature* (New York: W. W. Norton & Co., 1968) 1313.

thought or said, but to nature."[23] Huxley's prophetic utterances characterized the growing philosophical perspective and movement toward the replacement of a theological interpretation of the world with a naturalistic and secular one.

Philosophy, science, and theology were all unavoidably involved in the pervasive influence of Darwin's, *The Origin of Species*. By 1859, the date of *Origin's* publication, the way forward had already been philosophically prepared and the spirit of the times was receptive to Darwin's ideas. The philosophical development was instrumental in ushering in the empirical climate to receive the evolution hypothesis. Hegel's immanentistic developmentalism accompanied by Feuerbach's denial of the Creator/creation distinction and total rejection of a transcendent reality were both timely developments ushering the way for Darwin's speculative theory.

What was still needed, however, for the world to be better understood in naturalistic terms, was a system to integrate philosophy and science into a comprehensive system. Though some forms of philosophical and scientific evolution existed prior to Darwin, there was no plausible system explaining how it takes place. Darwin simply provided the naturalistic mechanism to the anti-transcendent processes already at work in speculative philosophy and theology. Darwin and Alfred R. Wallace (1823-1913) posed natural selection, or as it is commonly described, survival of the fittest, as the missing mechanism. In November of 1859, their position was made public in, *The Origin of Species*. As a result, within a decade, evolution became the accepted scientific orthodoxy. Naturalistic evolution, originally devised by Darwin to interpret his biological data, became the all-encompassing system by which numerous aspects of the universe could be explained.

The indomitable force of Darwinism soon transcended its biological beginnings and, as Dillenberger has noted, took upon itself the makings of a philosophical worldview. Huxley already understood his role as the

---

23 Huxley, "Science and Culture," 1313.

champion of naturalistic evolution proposing "the application of scientific methods of investigation to all the problems of life."[24] Another popularizer, Herbert Spencer (1820-1903), working in conjunction with Huxley, promoted Darwinism to the masses through the social sciences. It was largely through Spencer that Darwinism reached the person on the street. Spencer applied the Darwinian struggle for existence to every sphere of life. The power of the evolutionary process convinced him that nature ought not to be interfered with, and, therefore, he ought to oppose state education, poor laws, and housing reform.[25] Societies were viewed as organisms and social adaptation amid group struggle was the key to its survival. If humanity has evolved from animals, then it could be analyzed in biological categories.

The areas of acceptance increased. Not only did scientists entertain the plausibility of naturalistic evolution and its implications for all the sciences, but it drew the attention of biblical theologians as well. As the comprehensive concept of naturalism and evolution enlarged its circle of influence, it became clear that it was more than a biological theory. The broader implications expressed in the interpretation of scientific data led to serious concerns from the Christian community. Naturalism's inherent features presented themselves as principles for explaining the cause of existence, principles which the Christian tradition had claimed exclusive rights to for centuries. These were all worldview issues, rooted in presuppositions, and Christian theologians were not prepared or equipped to address them effectively. Consequently, the response to the new science and naturalism was hotly debated, leading to divisions in the Christian community not experienced since the sixteenth century.

By the time of the publication of Darwin's next work, *The Descent of Man*, in 1871, the unacceptable implications of speculative evolution for traditional Christianity had become apparent. To a large extent the issue

---

24   Huxley, "Science and Culture," 1314.

25   Colin Brown, *Philosophy and the Christian Faith*, 149.

had been reduced to the place of God within the naturalistic scheme, or if the God concept was even necessary at all. While the Newtonian view of a mechanical universe had a place for a Creator, the Darwinian view conceived nature as an unfinished process, thereby, eliminating the need for a Creator. Pearcey and Thaxton explain,

> By the end of the nineteenth century, mechanistic philosophy had become radically materialistic and reductionistic. It pictured living things as automata in a world governed by rigidly deterministic laws—with no purpose, no God, no significance to human life.[26]

Many recognized, through the successful efforts of Huxley, Spencer, Draper, and others, that the central doctrines of traditional Christian theism, the Genesis creation account, the nature of mankind, sin, the authority of the Bible, and even of God, were under serious attack.

As the debate expanded into the theological realm, sides were taken. Many just did not know how to deal with the concept of evolution and the naturalistic movement. Because presuppositions were involved that contained far-reaching theological implications, it was not easy to disentangle the various issues encountered. Polemics, which preceded any apologetic activity, dominated the theological discussion and eventually led to divisions.

With the exception of Benjamin Warfield and James Orr's adoption of a modified, or 'soft,' view on evolution, conservative theologians, however, resisted any compromise to the claims of naturalism. They did not concede that Christian theism involved only the aspects of things beyond scientific and historical inquiry. The influential Presbyterian theologian, Charles Hodge (1797-1878) of Princeton, arose as one of the few apologists able to confront Darwinism. Hodge, having studied the naturalists' work, understood their position and narrowed the real issue to a matter of

---

26   Pearcey and Thaxton, *The Soul of Science*, 116.

whether one believed in the intellectual process guided by God or a material process ruled by chance.[27] His understanding of the limitations of science was also apparent when he said, "science, as soon as she gets past the actual and the extant, is in the region of speculation, and is merged into philosophy, and is subject to its hallucinations."[28] His primary focus was on Darwin's view of natural selection without design. The idea that chance could generate design was, Hodge determined, rationally self-contradictory and, therefore, impossible. The heralded champion for the conservative Christian community concluded his masterful argument with the comment, "the denial of design in nature is virtually the denial of God."[29]

Warfield's adoption of evolution brought a great deal of credibility to the side of the new science. Along with Warfield (Hodge's successor at Princeton), Calvinists, Strong and Orr, also strengthened the position, but brought further division to the Christian community. Warfield's view of evolution, though modified, was, nonetheless, a form of evolution. He attempts to soften his view when he comments, "[t]he upshot of the whole matter is that there is no necessary antagonism of Christianity to evolution, provided that we do not hold to too extreme a form of evolution."[30]

Warfield clearly wanted to hold an evolutionary view and maintain the sovereignty of God within the process. James Orr, like Warfield, took a similar position when he remarked, "[o]n the general hypothesis of evolution, as applied to the organic world, I have nothing to say, except that, within certain limits, it seems to me extremely probable, and supported by a large body of evidence."[31] Later in the same work he declared, "[w]

27   Gregory, "The Impact," 376.

28   Charles Hodge, *Systematic Theology, Vol. II* (Grand Rapids: Eerdmans Publishing Co., [1873] 1968) 22.

29   Hodge, "Systematic Theology," 21.

30   Benjamin B. Warfield, "Lectures on Anthropology" (Speer Library, Princeton University, 1888) quoted in David N. Livingstone, *Darwin's Forgotten Defenders* (Grand Rapids: Wm B. Eerdmans Publishing Co., 1987) 118.

31   James Orr, *The Christian View of God and the World* (Grand Rapids: Kregel Publications, 1989) 99.

e need not reject the hypothesis of evolution within the limits in which science has really rendered it probable."[32]

But, as Frederick Gregory has noted, conservatives in general failed to develop a positive theology that effectively dealt with the issue after Darwin. As a result, attention increasingly shifted away from the conservative and evangelical groups and toward a more liberal treatment and acceptance of the evolutionary theory.[33] This harmonious acceptance was not going totally unnoticed by Christian conservatives, however, but few were willing to take on the momentum that had begun. Others were uninterested, believing that the Christian message would not or could not be affected by the changing scientific views. Gregory comments,

> As the scientific revolution progressed and a compromise seemed inevitable, numerous middle positions appeared attempting to reconcile Christian faith with modern intellectual trends. Three reconciliation views emerged. The first view held that by importing evolution into theology, while it would change some things, would not alter orthodoxy substantially. Others were less concerned about maintaining traditional Christian doctrine, but more in favor of adapting doctrine to the changing times. And still others made evolution the cornerstone of their theological perspective and Christian expression.[34]

For modernity, the naturalistic paradigm became the interpretive scheme applicable for all experience including the biblical tradition. The light of current knowledge was necessary to properly arrive at the essence of Christian doctrine. Naturalistic hermeneutics and higher historical criticism were adopted and employed to achieve that end. Within this context, the Genesis account of creation was understood to be a poetic account of

---

32   Orr, *The Christian View of God*, 182.

33   Gregory, "The Impact," 378.

34   Gregory, "The Impact," 379.

the goodness of God and the dependence of mankind upon God. Since humanity is in the process of change and development through an increase in knowledge, sin was viewed as mythological and identified with immaturity and insufficient knowledge. Humanity, for the naturalist, is essentially good, but due to the lack of knowledge, unfortunate things happen in the world. Additionally, scripture was no longer considered the authoritative word of God, as traditional Christian theism had believed and taught, but a record of growing religious awareness accomplished through an evolutionary process, which would ultimately lead to the kingdom of God on earth.

Because it encouraged investigation into a society's processes of change and development, the evolutionary model gained immediate acceptance in the academy. The result was an interpretive scheme in which institutions, cultures, and belief systems (religions), were also viewed as evolving. Within twenty years Darwinism and the evolutionary philosophy dominated all academic disciplines. It was an absolute triumph of a radical new idea that captured the minds of scholars and eventually the masses. The evolution hypothesis became the structural framework and the mechanism from which to interpret all of cultural life. It became the presuppositional principle for explaining organic relationships as well as behavioral causes. Sociologist, Robert Bellah[35], notes that though religious evolution was evident in classical times it was not until the nineteenth century that elaborate schemes of religious evolution with copious empirical illustration were developed by Hegel, Comte, and Spencer. In more modest and judicious form, evolutionary ideas provided the basis for the early sociology of religion of Emile Durkheim and Max Weber.[36]

35   Robert Bellah, *Beyond Belief: Essays on Religion in a Post-Traditional World* (New York: Harper and Row Publishers, 1970)

36   See Emile Durkheim, *The Elementary Forms of Religious Life*, trans. Karen Fields (New York: The Free Press, 1995 [1912]) and Max Weber, *The Sociology of religion*, trans. Ephraim Fischoff (Boston: Beacon Press, 1964 [1922]).

The theistic worldview, fractured from the effects of Enlightenment thought, was overwhelmed by the impact of the forceful new naturalistic philosophy. Evolutionary Darwinism split traditional Christianity rendering it ineffective and virtually unable to defend the traditional view against the momentum of this formidable foe. Though its decline had already begun, nineteenth century Christian theism as the reigning cultural beacon was progressively conquered and replaced by modernity's new speculative theory. In Kuhnian terms, Darwinism produced a genuine philosophical, theological, and cultural paradigm shift.

For the most part, modern Christian theology appropriated naturalism and the concept of evolution, resulting in new vitality and expansion. The theological ethos was different, however. Until the end of the nineteenth century, Christian theism was the dominant theology and intellectual force in most areas of life in Western culture. It was the view of the majority and not a marginalized minority. It was, in effect, the public religion and world view of the West. But after the turmoil of the late nineteenth century, the Christian view lost its hold as a shared, public commitment and retreated to the realm of private, individual belief.[37] As Dillenberger has rightly assessed, Christian theism had been superseded by an alternative philosophical worldview, which had won the exclusive right to delineate and interpret nature and experience. All views in opposition to naturalism were viewed as similar to Christian theism, that is, supernatural, and therefore relegated to the category of religion. Naturalism was clearly successful, but the question can be asked, was it due to the soundness of its argument or the weakness of the opposition? Was naturalism demonstrated to be rationally justified or did the 'climate of opinion'[38] overwhelm theism? These questions still need to be answered.

---

37   Pearcey and Thaxton, *Soul of Science*, xii.

38   This phrase was borrowed from chapter one of Carl Becker's, *The Heavenly City of the Eighteenth-Century Philosophers* (New Haven: Yale University Press, 1932).

4.2 Christian Theism's Response to Naturalism

Historian, George Marsden, would not disagree with Dillenberger, Coulson, and Kuhn, but goes a step further by attempting to uncover the reasons why the theistic worldview was replaced and what part apologetics played, or failed to play, in the process. He notes that recent historians of Darwinism largely agree that the early decades after *Origin of Species* the 'warfare' framework for understanding the relationship between Christianity and Darwinism was promoted primarily by ardent opponents of Christianity. In spite of the fact that earlier in the century Christians had been supporters of scientific progress, the anti-Christian polemicists claimed this to be another instance of the long-standing war between faith and science.[39]

In his incisive essay, *The Collapse of American Evangelical Academia,* Marsden discusses the intellectual components that led to the late nineteenth century demise of conservative evangelical academia and scholarship in the face of progressing modern naturalism.[40] He underscores the severity of the issue with the question, "Why was the severance of evangelicalism from the main currents of American academic life so total?"[41] The answer Marsden gives is complex, but centers on epistemology, particularly classical foundationalism, and the effect it had on theistic

---

39   George Marsden, *Understanding Fundamentalism and Evangelicalism* (Grand Rapids: Eerdmans Publishing Co., 1991) 122-52.

40   George Marsden, "The Collapse of American Evangelical Academia," in *Faith and Rationality,* eds. Alvin Plantinga and Nicholas Wolterstorff (Notre Dame, Ind.: University of Notre Dame Press, 1983) For additional discussion on this topic see D.G. Hart, ed., *Reckoning With the Past: Historical Essays on American Evangelicalism from the Institute for the Study of American Evangelicals* (Grand Rapids: Baker Books, 1995), George Marsden and Bradley Longfield, eds., *The Secularization of the Academy* (New York: Oxford University Press, 1992), Mark Noll, *The Scandal of the Evangelical Mind* (Grand Rapids: Eerdmans Publishing Co, 1994).

41   Marsden, "The Collapse of American Evangelical Academia," 221.

apologetics and its confrontation with nineteenth century modernity.[42] He argues that with the rise of modern natural science two alternative apologetic responses developed; the approach of Old Princeton, which Marsden believes aligned itself with evangelical evidentialism, and the presuppositional approach of Dutch theologian, Abraham Kuyper (1837-1920). These traditions, says Marsden, "are two of the strongest influences on current American evangelical thought on faith and reason."[43] A response to the rise of Naturalism came from both of these traditions and the following will briefly delineate how they each fared. Both responses contributed to the further development of the modern religion/science dichotomy and paradigm.

By the mid-nineteenth century two separate strands of Protestant theology impacted Christianity's defensive strategies against naturalism and emerged within the conservative tradition—one American and the other Dutch. These strands were an addition to the apologetic work previously developed and employed within conservative theology. The American strand, as we have already seen in the discussion of Nancey Murphy, found paramount expression in the organization of Princeton Theological Seminary in 1812, which, through the influence of Scottish philosopher/theologians, Thomas Reid (1710-1796), and James McCosh (1811-1894) became the center of conservative American theology.[44]

---

42 Marsden's thesis is not without opposition. See Donald Fuller and Richard Gardiner, "Reformed Theology At Princeton And Amsterdam In The Late Nineteenth Century," *Presbyterian: Covenant Seminary Review*, (21/2, 1995): 89-117 and Paul Helseth, "B. B. Warfield's Apologetical Appeal To 'Right Reason': Evidence of a Rather Bald Rationalism?" *Scottish Bulletin of Evangelical Theology, 16.2* (Autumn 1998): 156-77. Marsden's view on Old Princeton's "alleged" agreement with Enlightenment apologetic methodologies has been much debated. Marsden considers Old Princeton to be aligned with evangelical evidentialism. It is not the purpose of this essay, however, to enter this debate, but rather to show that the Dutch tradition perceived a difference and approached apologetics accordingly attempting to break from any type of evidentialism.

43 Marsden, "The Collapse," 247.

44 See J. David Hoeveler, *James McCosh And The Scottish Intellectual Tradition* (Princeton, NJ: Princeton University Press, 1981).

The Scottish Enlightenment, with its opposition to skepticism and revolution, promoted a Common Sense commitment to science, rationality, order, and the Christian tradition that dominated American academic thought for most of the nineteenth century.[45] Professors Archibald Alexander, Charles and A.A. Hodge, and Benjamin Warfield embraced this epistemic Common Sense Realism as the philosophical underpinning for the Old Princeton theology and specifically apologetics. Abraham Kuyper, following the Dutch, or continental Reformed tradition, inspired the other strand that eventually led to his founding of the Free University of Amsterdam in 1880. His immediate successors and legacy included Herman Bavinck and G.C. Berkouwer.

The significance of these two developments within the conservative theological tradition is in their respective dealings with modernity, particularly with their apologetic methodologies. Just as the larger movements— liberal and conservative—found it necessary to confront the culture differently due to philosophical perspectival differences, philosophical, or perhaps more appropriate, theological, assumptions also divided conservative Christians even further.

Marsden offers a plausible explanation as to why this split on defensive strategies occurred. He argues that the epistemic foundationalism of Thomas Reid guided Old Princeton's confrontation with the emerging naturalistic worldview. With this development Old Princeton had essentially aligned itself with the epistemic evidentialism of evangelicalism. The Kuyperian alternative, however, was not influenced by Reid and, therefore, did not encounter the same methodological issues.[46] They each addressed the naturalism of modernity differently, from their respective epistemologies. How each expression worked itself out will be summarized in the following.

---

45 Marsden, *Understanding Fundamentalism*, 128.

46 See Marsden, "The Collapse," and Nancey Murphy, *Anglo-American Postmodernity*, 87-112, Nancey Murphy, *Beyond Liberalism and Fundamentalism*.

As discussed above, originally theism and scientific reasoning were not at odds, but were complementary. But, "[w]hy was this view," asks Marsden, "once dominant in American higher education, so preemptively banished from most of American academia?"[47] The answer, he concludes, was that "their accommodation of Protestantism to science...was 'superficial.'" They did not "closely examine or challenge the speculative basis on which the modern scientific revolution was built."[48] Marsden draws heavily from an essay by Princeton philosopher, James Ward Smith, "Religion and Science in American Philosophy,"[49] to make the point of Protestantism's superficiality. In this essay Smith argues that their accommodation amounted to uncritically adding the findings of science to the existing corpus of biblical theology. The conclusions of modern science were simply viewed as additional support for the theistic argument from design.

This approach was superficial because compatibility between Christian theism and modern science was assumed without challenging modern science's presuppositions, or first principles. Rather, Christian theists uncritically adopted them insisting that objective scientific inquiry would only confirm Christian truth.[50] They failed to understand the shift in the metaphysical base that had taken place. The failure to recognize the inherently different foundational basic beliefs and the need for the rational justification of them, as well as for their own, eventually led to the conclusion that a biblical or theological perspective was irrelevant for the empirical sciences. Additionally, an effective natural theology had also waned, failing to address the issue of proof for the most basic belief of theism, the existence of God. The existence of God was dogmatically presupposed (fideism) and it could not withstand the challenges of empiricism.

---

47   Marsden, "The Collapse," 222.

48 Marsden, "The Collapse," 223.

49   James Ward Smith and A. Leland Jamison, eds. *The Shaping of American Religion* (Princeton: Princeton University Press, 1961) 402-42.

50   Marsden, "The Collapse," 223.

4.3 A Common Sense Response

The evangelical apologists believed that provided reason, or common sense, was allowed to prevail, the raw data of nature could be interpreted in an unbiased manner and thus establish the credibility of the Bible. For instance, the moral laws observable in nature serve to confirm the moral laws found in the Bible; hence, the author of the natural laws of the universe is also the author of the Bible.[51] But in doing so, Marsden argues, they assumed the naturalist's view of neutrality in their approach to empirical principles. Marsden explains that the leading evangelical spokesmen of the day, Francis Wayland, president of Brown University, and evangelical teacher, Mark Hopkins, led the charge with their two level approach to truth.

Wayland, who was a popular textbook author, claimed that rational moral science operating independently of Scripture will, unmistakably, reveal congruent principles. God's special revelation will always harmonize with natural law. Additional written revelation is necessary to supplement what reason already uncovers in principle. The approach was to assume the total objectivity of the scientific program and then point to the harmonies of scientific truth and the truth in the higher realms of religion and morality, thus "proving" Christianity's truth claims.[52]

Mark Hopkins' method was virtually identical to Wayland's. He believed and taught that the Bible reveals the same God that is known in nature. If the 'facts are properly authenticated' and viewed impartially, then the clear evidence will produce the certain proof of the Christian religion. So, in effect, the congruence of the biblical truth claims can be

---

51 Marsden, "The Collapse," 230-3.

52 Marsden, *Understanding Fundamentalism*, 132-3. Marsden argues that American Protestants of all sorts adopted a two-tiered worldview, founded on an empiricist epistemology, with laws of nature below, supporting supernatural belief above. He considers this a modern version of the Thomistic synthesis of reason and faith. He also points to H. Richard Niebuhr's "Christ above culture" intellectual framework in which the realism of science and faith could not conflict. 130-1.

tested with this intuitive and indisputable knowledge. Hopkins held to the prevailing opinion that our minds were endowed with innate powers that inevitably lead to certain beliefs. The commonality of these powers and beliefs throughout the race, which also included reason, established the 'common ground' from which philosophy and the proof of Christianity could proceed. Showing that what the Bible reveals is fully consistent with what we already know through natural revelation was the basis for Hopkins' apologetic. Hopkins' argument is similar to Joseph Butler's in pointing to the many analogies between the two revelations.[53]

The evangelical evidentialists claimed to start with a neutral objective epistemology upon which all could agree by common sense. This view worked as long as there was cultural consensus on metaphysical presuppositions. It was presumption, however, by the evangelical apologists to assume that these first principles were apparent to the entire human race and that everyone should agree to them.

It was also assumed that any rational investigation of the scientific data would prove theism and the biblical truth claims. The problem is there are a number of different interpretive constructs that could qualify as rational. The difference, of course, is the starting point—the presupposition. A case in point was Darwinism's removal of the presumed intelligent design of nature and hence the intelligent designer. Assuming a different starting point, Darwinism interpreted the data without an intelligent designer. Naturalists, following Laplace, had no need for the God hypothesis.

The principal Old Princeton apologists, Charles Hodge and B.B. Warfield, revealing their dependence on Locke, Joseph Butler, William Paley, and Reid (and following the evangelical trend), insisted that the relationship between special and general revelation must coincide and any scientific investigation and accumulation of evidence would overwhelm-

---

53   Marsden, "The Collapse," 235.

ingly attest to that harmony.[54] But, once again, to argue along these lines is begging the question. The evidence is gathered and interpreted to support a given hypothesis—a hypothesis which has already been assumed. With an alternative hypothesis, the same evidence could be interpreted differently. Darwinism is an example of interpreting the data from an alternative hypothesis. The real issue is how to adjudicate between the two mutually exclusive views.

Hodge believed Darwin had denied design and first causes in the universe and was adamant in his affirmation that the denial of design in nature is virtually the denial of God. In Hodge's thinking natural selection precluded the need for design and first causes. Darwin's rejection of final causes, led Hodge to conclude "it is this feature of his system which brings it into conflict not only with Christianity, but with the fundamental principles of natural religion, it should be clearly established."[55] The dictates of common sense would prove the congruence of Christian claims with this intuitive and indisputable knowledge establishing the 'common ground' from which philosophy and the proof of Christianity could proceed. Hodge further maintains in his definition of theology that the Scriptures contain the *facts* and *truths* about the physical world and it is the task of theology "to collect, authenticate, arrange and exhibit in their internal relation to each other."[56]

The problem was that Hodge argued his position from within a cultural context that was generally metaphysically uniform. The public consciousness for the era was decisively Christian and accepted the idea of a rational God who created an intelligent world governed by natural law. Additionally, Christopher Kaiser explains, it is because humans reflect the same rationality by which God ordered creation that they can understand

54   Marsden, "The Collapse," 244.

55   Hodge, *What is Darwinism?*, 48,52.

56   Hodge, *Systematic Theology, Vol.1*, 1.

that order.[57] The conviction that nature is intelligible came from biblical principles and as Carl Becker has noted; "[s]ince God is goodness and reason, his creation must somehow be, even if not evidently so to finite minds, good and reasonable. Design in nature was thus derived *a priori* from the character which the Creator was assumed to have."[58] Becker continues to explain that the idea of natural law for Christians was derived from belief in God prior to observation and was not derived *from* observation. That natural law exists was a fact of faith and not of experience.[59]

Building on this point, Pearcey and Thaxton note, whereas formerly the existence of God was regarded as so certain that it could serve as the starting point for argument, now it was the orderliness of nature, discovered by science that was regarded as more certain. Order in nature became the starting point of argument, and the existence of God became an inference from it, hence, the argument from design. This points to the massive intellectual shift that had taken place.[60]

The weakness of the evidentialist apologetics of Old Princeton, explains Marsden, was not in their "common sense assumptions and principles, but in their failure to recognize that a good many other assumptions were in fact functioning in their thought."[61] These other foundational assumptions were the points at which the apologetic method was constructed and the points where most vulnerable. Marsden contends that the apologetic response to this development from Old Princeton involved a defect in the American evangelical method of reconciling faith and science. The defects became apparent in three specific areas. The first was the immense confidence they had in the possibility of establishing most

---

57   Christopher Kaiser, *Creation and the History of Science* (Grand Rapids: Eerdmans Publishing Co., 1991) 127.

58   Carl Becker, *The Heavenly City of the Eighteenth-Century Philosophers* (New Haven: Yale University Press, 1932) 55.

59   Becker, *The Heavenly City*, 56-7.

60   Pearcey and Thaxton, *Soul of Science*, FN 28, 252.

61   Marsden, "The Collapse," 243.

of one's knowledge objectively. Second, they were sure that the common sense certainties of Baconian science could achieve certain conclusions compelling to any unbiased observer in most areas of human inquiry. Their third assumption was that nature is ordered, intelligible, and meaningful.[62] These assumptions (essentially the list Coulson ascribed to natural science) were manifest in Old Princeton's appeal to evidence in the world and they failed to address, or indeed even recognize, their interpretive and perspectival nature.

Marsden's criticism of Old Princeton and the evangelicals is essentially that there is no wholly neutral epistemic foundation or universally accepted rational scheme from which to judge reality objectively. All such judgments unavoidably contain metaphysical presuppositions by which a rational structure is constructed.[63] Neither of these points was recognized by the Christian evidentialists.

The Netherlands on the other hand, not having been influenced by enlightened modernity to the same degree as other western countries, experienced the least loss in traditional and evangelical Protestantism to intellectual science and secularism.[64] Hendrikus Berkhof explains that the Netherlands had remained somewhat isolated from modern theology until the mid-nineteenth century. At about the same time the Neo-Confessional theology of Kuyper appeared as a late response to the intellectual challenge of the Enlightenment.[65] Consequently, the Dutch Calvinists did not make the same philosophical assumptions with respect to foundationalism and evidential apologetics. Wolterstorff notes their "revulsion

---

62   Marsden, "The Collapse," 224, 241-2.

62   Marsden, "The Collapse," 224, 241-2.

63   Marsden, "The Collapse," 246-7.

64   Marsden, "The Collapse," 247 See also James D. Bratt, ed., *Abraham Kuyper: A Centennial Reader* (Grand Rapids: William Eerdmans Publishing Co., 1998) 3

65   Hendrikus Berkhof, *Two Hundred Years of Theology* (Grand Rapids: William Eerdmans Publishing Co.1989) 97-114

against arguments in favor of theism or Christianity" and their tendency to be "antievidentialist."[66]

Kuyper also recognized the need for first principles, but his approach was different than Reid and Old Princeton. It was his intention to distance himself from the evidentialists. He had difficulty accepting the concept of an objective scientific knowledge universally accessible to all intelligent humans. He did, though, accept that subjective perceptions of reality can correspond to an actual reality external to the individual, but the acceptance of a more primal belief must come first—belief in God as Creator.[67] God as Creator and sustainer was Kuyper's first principle.

Aware of Old Princeton's shortcomings, Kuyper noted that Hodge was choosing "*the facts of the Bible* as the object of his theology" and seeking authentication for them rather than constructing his theology on God the Creator as his first principle.[68] The problem with this approach, says Kuyper, is that "The authentication of his 'facts' brought him logically back again under the power of naturalistic science."[69] "His combination of 'facts and truths' overthrows his own system. He [Hodge] declares that the theologian must *authenticate* these truths. But then, of course, they are no *truths*, and only become such, when I authenticate them."[70] Kuyper's point here is that there exists a deep boundary line between theology and all other sciences. The object of the natural sciences is the creation, but the object of theology is the Creator, and the data of natural science does not authenticate the knowledge of the Creator, but the knowledge of the Creator is necessary for the authentication of science.[71]

---

66   Nicholas Wolterstorff, "Introduction," in *Faith and Rationality*, 7, 8

67   Abraham Kuyper, *Principles of Sacred Theology*, Trans. J. Hendrik De Vries (Grand Rapids: Baker Book House, 1980 [1898]) 241-292, 319-19

68   Kuyper, *Principles*, 318-19

69   Kuyper, *Principles*, 319

70   Kuyper, *Principles*, 318

71   Kuyper, *Principles*, 319

Contrary to Hodge and Warfield and the evangelical evidentialists, Kuyper does not understand belief in God and objective reality to be the conclusion of an inductive argument. The issue is the starting point. Any harmonious scientific correspondences between the subject and the external world must first *begin* with the Creator/creature distinction, as the presupposition. For Kuyper, "doing science...presupposed a whole theory about the fundamental structures of the universe."[72] His was what W.V.O. Quine would later call a "holistic" approach.[73]

Kuyper not only believed that Christian theism begins with first principles, but alternative life-systems do as well. An illustration of this point is Kuyper's understanding of the naturalist's theory of evolution. Prior to the dogma of evolution, says Kuyper, Christianity was the only life-system that bound all things into a single unity. But, with evolution and its absolute principle, monistic mechanics, its adherents could explain the entire cosmos, including all life processes within that cosmos, to the very earliest origins. This alternative is an all-encompassing system, a world-and-life view derived from a single principle.[74] The adherents, explains Kuyper, "now have a ground-dogma, and they cling to that dogma with unshakeable faith."[75]

Thomas Kuhn would consider this revolution as a change of world-view and a paradigm shift on a grand scale. As a result, says Kuhn, "scientists with different paradigms engage in different concrete laboratory manipulations."[76] Additionally, it should not be considered possible that these two life-systems can share and work from common principles. On

---

72   Marsden, "The Collapse," 253

73   See W.V.O. Quine and J.S. Ullian, *The Web of Belief* (New York: Random House, 1970) and Quine's "Two Dogmas of Empiricsm," in *From a Logical Point of View*, 2nd ed. (Cambridge, Mass.: Harvard University Press, 1953)

74   Abraham Kuyper, "Evolution," in *Abraham Kuyper: A Centennial Reader*, ed. James Bratt (Grand Rapids: Eerdmans Publishing Co., 1998 [1899]) 405-6

75   Kuyper, "Evolution," 406

76   Kuhn, *The Structure*, 126

the contrary, says Kuyper, "[t]he Christian religion and the theory of evolution are two mutually exclusive systems…antipodes that can be neither reconciled nor compared."[77] This antithesis formed the basis for much of Kuyper's thought.

Kuyper maintained that there are two kinds of people and two kinds of science. What he meant by this was that there are Christians and non-Christians in the world and "sin creates a widespread abnormality" affecting orientation and perspective. His apologetic represented more of an implementation of perspective, or "life system," as he called it, within the culture, rather than an appeal to evidence and argument.[78] As Prime Minister of the Netherlands between 1901 and 1905 he attempted to put his views into practice as the antidote to modern naturalism.

The difference between these two kinds of people and two kinds of science is in their faith. Not that one has faith and the other does not, but faith is a common denominator with the difference consisting in the content of the faith. Kuyper universalizes the concept of faith with the assertion that faith is a structural part of universal human nature.[79] In other words, Kuyper understood that all people begin their science with a first principle based in faith. First principles are basic beliefs held by faith, that is, without demonstration or proof. So the Christian as well as the naturalist begins his science from a first principle believed without rational justification. In this sense, both views are fideistic. The first principles of these two kinds of people, however, are radically different. The Christian begins with the presupposition that God is and he has created the world. The naturalist begins with an abstract notion of contingency—that the evidence may possibly point to a Creator—or may not. It is not clear to reason or any other kind of evidence whether God exists or not.

---

77   Kuyper, "Evolution," 412

78   Kuyper, *Principles*, 150-180

79   Kuyper, *Principles*, 125-6

As a precursor to Coulson, Dillenberger, Kuhn, and others who have recognized that knowledge and theoretical thought is grounded in metaphysical presuppositions, Kuyper argues for the concept of faith as a formal function of epistemology. He builds his case on three points. His first point is whether sense data received through empirical investigation of the world accurately corresponds to reality. Since there is no way to prove this proposition absolutely, then to believe that it does, as most, if not all scientists do, is an act of faith. Secondly, axioms are presupposed as valid concepts for the construction of theoretical knowledge. For example, the notion of non-contradiction as a basic rule of logic cannot be proven true or false without assuming the rule in the proof. Therefore, axioms of logic are assumed to be trustworthy without demonstration.

Kuyper's third point for establishing the universal nature of a faith structure is that universal statements derived from specific investigation and determined to be a general law are not based on the conclusions of the investigation, but are in fact presupposed prior to the investigation. "Without faith in the existence of the general in the special, in laws which govern this special, and in your right to build a general conclusion on a given number of observations," argues Kuyper, "you would never come to acknowledge such a law."[80] His understanding of faith provides the basis for certitude with respect to sense data, axiomatic inferences or deductions, and the application of general laws deduced from specific demonstrations.

From Kuyper's perspective, faith, then, as a general category, is a formal function and is the prerequisite for all knowledge and understanding. With this position, Kuyper is voicing St. Augustine's dictum "I believe in order to understand." Contrary to the naturalist's belief, the scientific method is not value neutral and objective with respect to the data of investigation, but begins with a faith based judgment. Faith then, for Kuyper, is not categorically relegated to the domain of religious, unverifiable knowl-

---

80   Kuyper, *Principles*, 139

edge only, but functions as an unproven presupposition and starting point for all views.

Neither of the theistic responses just discussed presented a significant challenge, or defeater, for naturalism. At best with these two responses, theism and naturalism may be considered equivalent, but with no way to determine one or the other to be more rational or privileged. Kuyper's argument established all views as fideistic in their most basic beliefs and, therefore, a basis for being incommensurate. A means to determine which view has knowledge and certainty is not to be found in any view. Faith is not knowledge, however. If first principles are derived from faith, as Kuyper maintains, then how is it determined which first principles produce knowledge and certainty? It appears that skepticism is the only logical conclusion. No view can be rationally determined to be any better than another. That is, no view can be determined to be true or false, right or wrong, or good or evil. A valid argument could be made that Kuyper's understanding had already anticipated the intellectual trend that would come to be called postmodernity.

4.4 Summary

The preceding has highlighted how Enlightenment ideals found their way into the mainstream of modern life and how some key Christian theologians responded. As Stow Persons has noted, the synthesis formed by the three ideological currents of the Protestant Reformed tradition, democratic social ideology, and naturalistic philosophy has resulted in an intellectual matrix that produced the modern secular age. An effort was made in the above to focus primarily on the third aspect of this multi-faceted movement—the rise of naturalism—and its transformational effect in producing the modern worldview. The impact was controversial indeed and not without a diverse reaction from the philosophical and theistic communities.

The extraordinary success of new scientific hypotheses in the nineteenth century had truly ushered in the age of positivism characterized by a supreme 'faith in science' which, according to physicist/philosopher, C.F. von Weizsacker, had replaced faith in religion.[81] Faith in science was merely another way of stating the exclusive role science had achieved as the authoritative producer of certainty and knowledge building on the foundation set by Descartes and Locke. This knowledge was experienced in the practicality of modern science as it acquired more and more relevance for everyday life. What was originally considered a war of principles ultimately gave way to the practical and an empirically rooted philosophy of pragmatism. In keeping with the vision of French philosopher, Auguste Comte (1798-1857), the intellectual revolution had entered its third phase—the positive stage, following theology and metaphysics of earlier ages—where observation and measurement of phenomena is the highest development of the intellect. Whether this particular understanding of the scientific revolution is accepted or not, the empiricism of the late nineteenth and early twentieth century, nevertheless, generated a substantive redirection in philosophy and theology.[82]

Naturalism brought about change in the intellectual climate. The natural sciences had a way of subsuming all other disciplines. The strength of empiricism challenged the meaning and purpose of philosophy and even the existence of a metaphysical reality. Theology, of course, was on the endangered species list.[83] Natural science initiated a host of new critically reflective thought that influenced both philosophy and so-called religion.

The new science created a cultural consciousness receptive to the idea that an empirical test as verification for knowledge was a logical conclu-

---

81   C.F. von Weizsacker, *The Relevance of Science* (London: Collins, 1964) 13.

82   For additional discussion on this issue in philosophy during this period see Ayer, Kneale, Paul, Pears, Strawson, Warnock, and Wolleim, eds. *The Revolution in Philosophy* (London: Macmillan & Co. Ltd., 1960, and in theology see Flew and MacIntyre, eds. *New Essays in Philosophical Theology* (London: SCM Press Ltd., 1955).

83   For a summary of the new direction of philosophical theology see Flew and MacIntyre, *New Essays in Philosophical Theology*, (New York: Macmillan & Co., 1964).

sion in the quest for a normative science. Thus, the later developments of the Vienna Circle and A.J. Ayer, building on the progression of nineteenth century positivism in science, concluded that anything other than the empirical is non-verifiable. Essentially, observation was deemed the only solid foundation for all knowledge. This proposition led Ayer to expound that no type of speculative knowledge about the world is, in principle, beyond the scope of empirical science. Analytical reflection on metaphysics, therefore, is nothing short of a delusion.[84] With the relegation of the exploration of empirical fact to the various special sciences, the investigation of a transcendent metaphysical realm becomes fruitless and illusory. The task of the new philosophy was to only clarify propositions of language since traditional philosophy could not report on matters of fact and satisfy the newly formulated requirements of either inductive or deductive science.[85]

Discovery of the profound truths of the universe no longer needed the insights of theoretical philosophical thought. Metaphysics was deemed irrelevant due to the belief that knowledge of ultimate reality was not possible. Needless to say, naturalism as a life-system and worldview had reached hegemonic proportions and had a radical impact on philosophy and theology.

Having taken this direction, philosophy and theology then lost their ability to speak authoritatively on questions about the being of God and the universe and became simply an analysis of the logical procedures of language and description.[86] Ayer's particular brand of empiricism was short-lived, however. Many saw what John Macquarrie observed, "'[n]aturalism' is itself a metaphysic—it is the identification of reality with

---

84   Alfred J. Ayer, *Language, Truth and Logic* (New York: Dover Publications, Inc. ND) 48 Also, see John Macquarrie, *Twentieth Century Religious Thought* (New York: Harper & Row Publishers, 1963) 301-3.

85   See the introduction by Gilbert Ryle in *The Revolution in Philosophy*, 4-6.

86   Macquarrie, *Twentieth Century Religious Thought*, 301.

nature."[87] In spite of its critics, logical empiricism and analytical philosophy continued well into the twentieth century challenging the legitimacy of contemporary theology, apologetics, essentially the religion idea, and eventually philosophy itself. Logical positivism/empiricism was clearly an attempt to move away from Christian theistic principles and toward a more distinct philosophical naturalism.[88] As the discussion above attempts to show, with the progression of a naturalistic worldview the marginalization of Christian theism became more evident with little help from apologetic strategies.

Opposed to the notion that philosophy is solely the analysis of language, metaphysical realists looked for an explanation of reality that included more than just the human component claiming that metaphysics still has an important role. Accepting the speculative evolutionary process of the positivists, but unwilling to exclude God altogether, they developed a metaphysical model with God as part of the process. With the supernatural existence of God challenged, a non-supernatural theism inevitably emerged, replacing the idea of an immutable God with a God who is mutable and *becoming*.

In keeping with the naturalist outlook, Alfred N. Whitehead and Charles Hartshorne, metaphysical realists who identified God with the natural processes in the world, initiated various forms of a process concept. One popular theological expression is Hartshorne's proposal that God is an unchanging essence, but who completes himself in an advancing experience.

Since the emergence of Darwinism, the traditional concept of God has been all but vanquished. The understanding of God as infinite, eternal, and immutable as expressed in the seventeenth century's Westmin-

---

87 Macquarrie, *Twentieth Century Religious Thought*, 96.

88 Macquarrie notes that logical empiricism and the earlier version, logical positivism, shifted from a question of truth to the prior question of meaning. The question of God's existence became an issue about the 'meaning' of the word existence. For the non-Christian philosopher, propositions about the existence of God were not meaningful and therefore neither true nor false. *Twentieth Century Religious Thought*, 302.

ster Confession of Faith has been removed from the public domain. The emphasis shifted to a type of natural theology that synthesized temporal processes with an eternal essence.[89] Alvin Plantinga has identified logical positivism and particularly its subsequent allied streams of naturalistic thought as the most influential and most negative of theism's opponents in the early twentieth century.[90]

Though intense polemics subsided, subtle tension continued between naturalism, philosophy, and traditional theism about the question of knowledge—is it possible and what perspective can claim to have it. The faith versus reason controversy has been an on-going issue. For centuries the intellectual debate has tended to place faith in opposition to reason so it is not surprising that the distinction between religion and science has taken the representative roles of religion (faith) and science (reason). In keeping with Enlightenment ideals, modernity sided with the autonomy of natural science and placed faith on the irrelevant periphery, thus reinforcing the ostensible impenetrable dichotomy.

This new authoritative position of naturalism carries with it the responsibility of justifying its privileged position to the culture. It must rationally justify its claim to exclusive knowledge and truth. It must be more than a dogmatic claim—the charge leveled against theism. In keeping with modernity's conception of knowledge, it must demonstrate its truth claims, its foundational first principles, that the material world is all that exists and is the sole basis for understanding the nature of reality. This foundational basic belief provides the basis for the system of knowledge affirmed by philosophical naturalism. The naturalistic worldview is constructed on a type of 'first philosophy,' a Cartesian/Lockean foundation of 'clear and distinct' ideas that must be demonstrated. The next two chapters will explore how this effort fared in the twentieth century.

---

89   Macquarrie, *Twentieth Century Religious Thought*, 267-277.

90   Alvin Plantinga, "Christian Philosophy at the End of the Twentieth Century," in James F. Sennett, ed. *The Analytic Theist: An Alvin Plantinga Reader* (Grand Rapids: Eerdmans Publishing Co., 1998) 329.

5

A Critical Analysis
of a Modern Paradigm

THIS CHAPTER WILL focus on two items; one, to reveal the general
and contemporary philosophical context in which naturalism and religion are situated, and two, to explore this context in some detail as it
relates to questions of epistemology, the concept of rationality, and the
religion / science dichotomy. It will be necessary to gain a greater understanding of naturalism's position by exploring the philosophical developments and specific philosophers from the late nineteenth century to the
present, with an emphasis on epistemology.

As the twentieth century has clearly shown, naturalism has gained
predominance in the Western academy. Theism has been unable to successfully establish itself as a rational worldview in light of formidable challenges. The need for God and the supernatural (commonly understood
as the religious view), in the minds of many, could not be substantiated.
As a result, an alternative explanation of the nature of the world and experience won the day at the end of the nineteenth century. Naturalism
claimed Reason and verifiable evidence to make its case. Theism, on the
other hand, with its strong appeal to the special revelation of God (scrip-

ture) had difficulty establishing a rational basis for its beliefs. It needed to prove the existence of God, but could not, so it settled for a fideistic position—a most basic belief with no proof.

Assuming that God does exist, how then is this God known? If it is by scripture, then how is the correct scripture determined—a fair question. For naturalists, theism was thought to be belief that could not be rationally justified. At best, it could only be considered a fideistic belief system. And, at least since the Enlightenment period of Locke, Hume, and Kant, beliefs with no evidence had not only lost credibility, but also relevance.

As emphasized in earlier chapters, the fundamental issue between science and so-called religion is one of epistemology, how reality is known. Knowledge is the key here. Which view can claim knowledge and, therefore, truth? The issue is about the nature of these concepts. Is Reason capable of grasping knowledge and truth, and what qualifies as evidence of such? Descartes' notion of self-evident clear and distinct ideas and Locke's sensations that form a foundation of certainty, and thus replacing Reformation fideism, continues to be naturalism's answer.

The belief system of naturalism is constructed on a foundation that maintains that the material universe is all that exists. Sense data, then, is the sole and exclusive source of knowledge—empiricism. Observable data is all that can be clearly known. Remnants of logical positivism still persist. If it cannot be sensed by empirical analysis, then it cannot exist.

A materialist vision of the universe is not new, however.[1] From the ancient Greeks to the present the belief that the universe is in no need of divine guidance or origin has persisted. Naturalism's fundamental claims are that alternative non-material perspectives of the universe cannot be supported by reason or evidence. The charge against theism and religion in general has been, and still is, that they are non-cognitive and have no foundational first principle that can be supported with substantive evidence or proof. The idea of a transcendent reality is a human fabrication

---

1   James Thrower traces this thought progressively as an expression of atheism from the ancient times to the present in, *Western Atheism*.

and projection, it is argued. These kinds of claims in the modern era range from Ludwig Feuerbach's projectionist theory, to renowned twentieth century philosopher, Bertrand Russell's comment, "[t]he whole conception of God is a conception derived from the ancient Oriental despotisms," to eminent biologist, Richard Dawkins' repeat of the famous Laplace declaration, "there is no evidence to favour the God Hypothesis."[2]

Naturalism and its foundation of matter would not go unchallenged for long, however. Since the end of the nineteenth century at least two epistemological challenges have been put forth. Both question the foundation upon which naturalism is constructed. The first challenges the very idea of a foundation for knowledge and translates into what has come to be known as postmodernity. The postmodern ethos, mostly expressed in the academic disciplines of the social sciences and humanities, has found itself at odds with the physical sciences, which still holds to a foundation. This tension came to a head in what was called the 'science wars' of the 1990's. This is an on-going issue and has yet to be resolved.[3] The second challenge retains a foundation, but challenges naturalism's particular foundational beliefs. In what follows, the very ground upon which naturalism builds its case will be critically examined by two separate arguments. This chapter addresses the challenge to the idea of a foundation for thought and the next chapter addresses naturalism's specific foundational beliefs.

5.1 Deconstructing Modernity's Foundational Epistemology

By the estimation of many, modernity has run its course and has given way to philosophic challenges that have impacted all world view narratives. That the present era is in some sense 'postmodern' appears to be the

---

2   Bertrand Russell, *Why I Am Not a Christian* (New York: Simon & Schuster, 1957) 23. Richard Dawkins, *The God Delusion* (Boston: Houghton Mifflin, 2006) 83.

3   For an informative summary of this issue see Keith Parsons, ed. *The Science Wars: Debating Scientific Knowledge and Technology* (New York: Prometheus Books, 2003). See also, Michael Ruse, *Mystery of Mysteries: Is Evolution a Social Construction?* (Cambridge: Harvard University Press, 1999)

consensus. But as important as it may seem, no attempt at a definition of postmodernity will be made here other than to describe those features broadly related to epistemology.

Epistemic nonfoundationalism,[4] a philosophical criticism resulting from work in metaepistemology, precipitated new philosophical strategies in the twentieth century. Pluralism and deconstructionism are two ideologies that characterize the new era and are contending for an authoritative voice in the history of thought. Postmodernity is part of a continuum informed by the matured modern era and so must be examined in light of the modern. Though modernity can be assessed from many angles and intellectual disciplines, it is clear from the foregoing discussion that a central philosophical feature of modernity is epistemic foundationalism. It should be no surprise then that a nonfoundational epistemology represents a major tenet of the postmodern perspective.

Since the late nineteenth century much philosophical work from the naturalist tradition has, ironically, been offered in an effort to undermine the Cartesian/Lockean view of rationality and the assumptions of an epistemology of absolute knowledge.[5] All available philosophical artillery has been aimed directly at the foundation of non-inferentially known certitudes upon which Descartes and Locke's superstructure of knowledge was constructed.

Naturalism needs a foundational belief so it is ironic that inferences consistent with the foundational belief are being made by naturalist philosophers such as Willard Van Orman Quine who are actually intent on undermining the position. Locke and his foundation of certainty (and all

---

4   In his work, *Nonfoundationalism*, John Thiel comments that nonfoundationalism is not a position or stance in its own right but a judgment about what is *not* philosophically tenable. (Minneapolis: Fortress Press, 1994) 2.

5   Alvin Plantinga has noted that in the last quarter of the twentieth century naturalism has taken an increasingly aggressive and explicit stance. Naturalistic accounts are given on various philosophical topics and phenomena including epistemology, intentionality, morality, teleology, proper function, language, meaning, thought, and much more. "Christian Philosophy at the End of the Twentieth Century," in *The Analytic Theist: An Alvin Plantinga Reader* (Grand Rapids: Eerdmans Publishing Co., 1998) 330.

subscribers to it) has become the target for the arsenal of twentieth century philosophers like Quine, Wilfred Sellars, and Richard Rorty, each of
whom approaches the subject with empiricist inclinations.[6] For them,
indubitable foundations are in fact dubious, if not impossible, and have
been replaced with a paradigm of practical contextuality. Though these
three figures have had predecessors, they, arguably, form the nucleus of the
twentieth century assault on epistemic foundationalism upon which the
current naturalistic view is constructed. While the distinguished position
of philosophy has been challenged by postmoderns, its conclusions, nonetheless, have formed the basis for the philosophy of science and religion.[7]

With the favored epistemology of postmodernity underscored, a cur-
sory review of other related key features of this phenomenon will also be
of value here. An overview will highlight some salient modern and postmodern characteristics. Typically, postmodernity is identified by terms
like; 'relativism' with respect to ethics, truth, and meaning; a 'decentered'
humanity; and 'pluralistic' worldviews. In a broad sense these are reasonably accurate, however, a little more explanation will be helpful.

The first point that needs clarification is the present status of modernity. While modernity may be considered bankrupt by many today, it is

---

6   For works addressing foundationalism see Quine's *The Web of Belief*, Sellars' *Science, Percep-
     tion and Reality* (New York: Humanities Press, 1963) and Rorty's *Philosophy and the Mirror
     of Nature*.

7   The editors of *After Philosophy: End or Transformation*, Baynes, Bohman, and McCarthy have
     made some insightful comments in their introduction about the contemporary status of phi-
     losophy and themes representing the postphilosophical era. The rise of the modern sciences
     of nature, they say, removed—forever, it seems—vast domains from the authority of philo-
     sophical reflection. Postphilosophy is characterized by opposition to strong conceptions of
     reason and of the autonomous rational subject, the contingency and conventionality of the
     rules, criteria, and products of what counts as rational speech and action at any given time
     and place. They oppose the irreducible plurality of incommensurable language games and
     forms of life, the irremediably "local" character of all truth, argument, and validity, to the a
     priori the empirical, to certainty fallibility, to invariance historical and cultural variability, to
     unity heterogeneity, to totality the fragmentary, to self-evident givenness ("presence") uni-
     versal mediation by differential systems of signs, to the unconditioned a rejection of ultimate
     foundations in any form, transcendental conditions of possibility no less than metaphysical
     first principles. (Cambridge: The MIT Press, 1988) 1, 3.

not clear as to whether it has been superseded. The present is a time of cultural transition processing the inherent features and benefits of modernity against the genuinely novel postmodern elements. The extent to which postmodernity differs from modernity, in addition to the epistemic issue, is a topic of current debate. Is there a difference in kind or only in degree? Scholars such as Jurgen Habermas of the philosophical world, Wolfhart Pannenberg in theology, and John Rawls in moral and political theory have worked diligently to preserve the solvency of the modern project. More will be said below on the idea of preserving the modern project.

The Enlightenment's call to autonomous individuality has known no boundaries. The phenomenon seems to be omnipresent. Philosopher/theologian, Nancey Murphy, claims that the individualism of the Enlightenment manifested itself in the atomistic and reductionistic tendencies of early natural science and ultimately pervaded all aspects of modern thought. "The fragmented 'postmodern self,'" she argues, "is but a further atomization of the modern individual and was already discussed by David Hume."[8] Postmodern individualism is nothing new, she says. Perhaps the decentered or "fragmented" self is the product of human autonomy and is, therefore, an abiding continuum regardless of whether it manifests itself in modernity or postmodernity. Murphy goes on to say "what is called postmodern in contemporary Western culture is nothing but pure modernity finally hitting the streets."[9]

The idea of a continuum between modernity and postmodernity is also found with contemporary philosopher, Richard Rorty. Based on his contention that "postmodernity is characterized by the rejection of the Cartesian ideal and the radicalization of the Baconian,"[10] there seems to be strong justification for saying that "the postmodern is a continuance

---

8   Murphy, *Anglo-American Postmodernity*, 209.

9   Murphy, *Anglo-American Postmodernity*, 209.

10   Richard Rorty, *Objectivity, Relativism and Truth* (Cambridge: Cambridge University Press, 1991) 33, n.16. See the essays in part 1 for his critique of the Cartesian ideal and in part 2 for his defense of the Baconian ideal.

and *intensification* of (one aspect of) the modern."[11] The work of Descartes and Francis Bacon (1561-1626) converged to form an optimistic vision of the world and reality. What emerged was Descartes with his indubitable rational foundation for a science that corresponds to the external world, and Bacon, the popularizer, who saw knowledge as a powerful tool for controlling nature and improving the human condition. The combination offered the optimism of utopian values through objective realism and human autonomy.[12] What Rorty seems to be saying is that with the collapse of foundationalism the Cartesian ideal went along with it leaving Bacon's vision—the optimistic progress myth—except in a more radical form.

This progress myth is another overarching psychological characterization of modernity that continues to have considerable influence. Modernity still holds the appeal and promise of Cartesian realism and Baconian natural science. In his proposal for a philosophical interpretation of history, Gordon Graham argues that despite the twentieth century decline in optimism due to the world's wars and the collapse of the old colonial empires, "an argument can be advanced to show just how difficult it is to avoid some sort of progressivism."[13] A view that considers itself *better* than previous ones, which is the twentieth century opinion with respect to the nineteenth, is, in fact, a progressive view. Moreover, modern relativists cannot avoid considering their own view an improvement on the narrower thinking of the past.[14] Progressivism, even with its perspectival aspect, is, nonetheless, difficult to deny, affirming Graham's claim that "some sort of progressivism is hard to resist."[15]

---

11   J. Richard Middleton and Brian J. Walsh, *Truth Is Stranger Than It Used to Be: Biblical Faith in a Postmodern Age* (Downers Grove, Ill.: InterVarsity Press, 1995) 41.

12   Middleton, *Truth Is Stranger Than It Used to Be*, 41.

13   Gordon Graham, *The Shape of the Past: A Philosophical Approach to History* (Oxford: Oxford University Press, 1997) 46.

14   Graham, *The Shape of the Past*, 46-9.

15   Graham, *The Shape of the Past*, 49.

But there is more to modernity than the self-centered subject and the progress myth. The modern outlook has been shaped, not only by a spirit of individual freedom and optimism, but also by the autonomous quest for certitude, the absolutizing of the laws of nature (including reason), and the relegation of authority to the periphery, to mention just the major points.[16]

Postmodernity, however, is a phenomenon to reckon with in its own right. Theologian, Diogenes Allen, sees the present postmodern situation as "[a] massive intellectual revolution" where "[t]he foundations of the modern world are collapsing" and "[t]he principles forged during the Enlightenment...are crumbling."[17] In the postmodern environment much of contemporary intellectual inquiry has been shaped decisively by fragmentation, indeterminacy, and intense distrust of all universal or 'totalizing' discourses.

But, in the midst of the confusion surrounding postmodernity some believe that there are prominent signs that give reason for hope. Theologian, Stanley Grenz, argues that two aspects of the postmodern ethos are particularly significant; "the fundamental critique and rejection of modernity, and the attempt to live and think in a realm of chastened rationality characterized by the demise of modern epistemological foundationalism."[18] As diverse as the postmodern phenomenon is, there is unity among postmodern thinkers in their rejection of the modern project's quest for certain, objective, and universal knowledge, along with the hesitation to form rational paradigms for replacing the modern vision.

Grenz's first item, the unity in the rejection of modernity, plays out in various ways. Radical aspects can be found in continental deconstruction-

---

16   For modernity's quest for certitude see Stephen Toulmin, *Cosmopolis;* For God and the laws of nature in modernity see Bruno Latour, *We Have Never Been Modern;* and for modernity and authority see Jeffrey Stout, *Flight from Authority.*

17   Diogenes Allen, *Christian Belief in a Postmodern World: The Full Wealth of Conviction* (Louisville: Westminster/John Knox, 1989) 2

18   Stanley Grenz/John Franke, *Beyond Foundationalism: Shaping Theology in a Postmodern Context* (Louisville: Westminster John Know Press, 2001) 19.

ism, a literary theory, as represented by French critics Jacques Derrida and Jean-Francois Lyotard. Deconstructionism confronts the world with the claim that all order and convention is strictly arbitrary. This sounds like Toulmin's account of the French "clean slate" theory again with all vestiges of Descartes having been, ironically, authoritatively deconstructed. Any criteria for determining such characteristics as order and convention, explains Rorty, is itself a human construction—and there is "no standard of rationality that is not an appeal to such a criterion, no rigorous argumentation that is not obedience to our own conventions."[19] Even the very convention of language, a favorite topic for the deconstructionists, does not escape subjectivism, which undermines the biblical medium as a metanarrative. Lyotard has expressed his distrust of language to convey meaning and his related disdain for the metanarrative as a medium for meaning with his pointed definition of postmodernity, "[s]implified to the extreme, I define *postmodern* as incredulity toward metanarratives."[20]

Anthropologically, deconstructionists tend to celebrate human decenteredness and view it as a virtuous attribute. The irony, once again, in keeping with the tenets of postmodernity, is the decentered self. While perspectival in nature, decenteredness, still derives some sort of meaning, only within a particular context. Theologian, Mark C. Taylor, views the dissolution of the individual self as giving rise to "anonymous subjectivity" in which "care-less sacrifice takes the place of anxious mastery."[21] With the recurring appearance of Nietzsche, arguably the original deconstructionist, in the work of Taylor and the French deconstructionists, decenteredness could, perhaps, even be the line to the will to power and the *Ubermensch*. Deconstructionists, existentialists, and poststructuralists in

19   Richard Rorty, "Pragmatism and Philosophy," in *After Philosophy: End or Transformation?* ed. Kenneth Baynes, James Bohman and Thomas McCarthy (Cambridge, Mass.: MIT Press, 1987) 60.

20   Jean-Francois Lyotard, *The Postmodern Condition: A Report on Knowledge*, trans. G. Bennington and B. Massumi (Minneapolis: University of Minnesota Press, 1984) xxiv.

21   Mark C. Taylor, *Erring: A Postmodern A/Theology* (Chicago: The University of Chicago Press,1984) chap. 6.

general have drawn heavily from Nietzsche's thought, which opens the possibilities for various deconstructionist anthropologies.[22]

Though the term 'postmodern' has been most typically associated with continental thinkers and deconstructionism, it is, however, becoming more prevalent in other contexts. More 'conservative' or 'constructive' versions of postmodernity are emerging in America with philosophers and theologians such as Thomas Kuhn, Alistair MacIntyre, Stephen Toulmin, Jeffrey Stout, George Lindbeck, Ronald Thiemann, and Nicholas Wolterstorff, to name just a few. In the rejection of the tenets of modernity there is unity. The range in congruence, Grenz observes, "extends from Derrida to the so-called post-conservative evangelicals."[23]

The second aspect identified by Grenz as at the heart of the postmodern ethos, and of particular interest here, is the attempt in the aftermath of modernity to rethink the nature of rationality. He calls the result of the attempt, *chastened rationality*.[24] In retrospect, he argues, the faculty of reason, the exalted trademark of the Enlightenment, was given more power than it was due. Princeton theologian, Wentzel van Huyssteen, similarly understands the need to reconsider the limits of rationality when he says "postmodern thought also challenges us again to explore the presupposed continuity between Christian theology and the general human enterprise of understanding the world rationally."[25] Although postmodernity does not reject the concept of rationality, it does reject the Cartesian/Lockean starting point for it—an evaluative norm accessible to the mind. But in spite of Richard Rorty's objections, in this post-metaphysical age, episte-

---

22 For a detailed work on Nietzsche and the Deconstructionists see Alan D. Schrift, *Nietzsche's French Legacy: A Genealogy of Poststructuralism* (New York: Routledge, 1995).

23 Grenz, *Beyond Foundationalism*, 21.

24 Grenz, *Beyond Foundationalism*, 22-3.

25 J. Wentsel van Huyssteen, *Essays in Postfoundationalist Theology* (Grand Rapids: William B. Eerdmans Publishing Co., 1997) 217.

mology continues to be the focus of attention.[26] Rationality, its place and function, even if chastened, is inseparable from the pursuit of knowledge. Theoretical reason, Robert Audi has remarked, "is roughly the topic of epistemology."[27] The next chapter will further explore the popular idea of 'chastened reason' and whether it is a viable position.

Grenz identifies three categories affected by chastened rationality. The first is that humans do not view the world from an objective vantage point, but structure an understanding of it through the social convention of language. But due to the various perspectives of the speaker and the lack of a universal language for describing the 'real world,' no single linguistic description is adequate. The second is that the metanarrative is no longer credible as a universal shaper of the cultural ethos, but functions in a local context only. Diversity and plurality has replaced the notion of a grand scheme into which all particular stories must fit. The third, and possibly the most significant and prominent category of chastened rationality, is the collapse of epistemological foundationalism.[28] The Enlightenment view that rationality is determined by, and grounded in, self-evident, indubitable foundational beliefs that are trans-historical and fixed metaphysical entities, is not tenable in the postmodern context.

While it is the topic of epistemology, the difficulty in discussing reason or rationality in any absolute or reductionistic sense is as philosopher, Hilary Putnam, explains, "the 'standard' accepted by a culture or a subculture, either explicitly or implicitly, cannot *define* what reason is, even in context, because they *presuppose* reason (reasonableness) for their interpretation.[29] On the one hand, Putnam continues, reasonableness is

---

26   Rorty rejects the traditional integrity of philosophy and particularly epistemology. *Philosophy and the Mirror of Nature* (Princeton NJ: Princeton University Press, 1979).

27   Robert Audi, *The Architecture of Reason: The Sturcture and Substance of Rationality* (Oxford: Oxford Universtiy Press, 2001) 4.

28   Grenz, *Beyond Foundationalism*, 23.

29   Hilary Putnam, "Why Reason Can't be Naturalized," in *After Philosophy: End or Transformation?* eds. Baynes, Bohman, and McCarthy (Cambridge, Mass.: MIT Press, 1987) 228.

shaped by cultures, practices, and procedures and on the other hand, it has a universal aspect to it. For it is "both immanent (not to be found outside of concrete language games and institutions) and transcendent (a regulative idea that we use to criticize the conduct of all activities and institutions)."[30] In other words, reason is used to postulate anything about reason. It can be used incorrectly, but not denied without using it. Recognizing this dilemma and others, a new philosophy, pragmatism, was offered as a resolution.

5.2 The Rise of Coherentist Epistemology

An epistemological revolution, which began with the maturation of naturalism and represented by the philosophical pragmatism of Charles Sanders Peirce (1839-1914) and William James (1842-1910) of the early twentieth century, has continued through the logical empiricism of Bertrand Russell, Gottlob Frege (1848-1925), and Ludwig Wittgenstein (1889-1951), and finally to Willard Van Orman Quine, Wilfred Sellars, and Richard Rorty of the last half of the twentieth century. This trajectory of empirically based epistemology has impacted and left its mark with implications for naturalism and its foundation.

A postmodern precursor, pragmatic philosophy, initiated by Peirce and James and further developed in the twentieth century, reexamined the Enlightenment constitution of rationality. Pragmatism in philosophy undermined the prevailing Cartesian/Lockean tradition in three crucial areas, which represented the beginnings of nonfoundationalism as a philosophical criticism. The first was the rejection of the Cartesian method of establishing the first principles of philosophy as a necessary propaedeutic to philosophical inquiry itself. Second, the accepted metaphysics of understanding were rejected. As the foundation for the truth of a philosophical system, neither sense experience nor ideas were considered privileged as an authoritative basis of knowing. Thirdly, the rationalist or empiricist

---

30   Putnam, "Reason," 228.

definition of truth as an isolated correspondence between self and world was also rejected. In its place was the understanding that truth is found in a social context of meaning shaped by the practical implications of ideas. The contextual and foundationless aspect of pragmatism then led to disparate epistemological expressions including Wittgenstein's 'linguistic turn' in which language was viewed as the vehicle for meaning,[31] and, additionally of particular importance for naturalism, Thomas Kuhn's 'normal science' working within a framework of an accepted paradigm.

Directing his charge at the spirit of Cartesianism in an 1868 essay, Peirce concluded that "[w]e have no power of Intuition," that "every cognition is determined logically by previous cognitions," and that, because there is "no power of thinking without signs," there is no logical reason for positing some foundational point of departure for this intellectual process.[32] Along similar lines of argument Wittgenstein observed in his later work that philosophy "may in no way interfere with the actual use of language; it can only describe it...[and] it cannot give it any foundation either."[33] Language, for Wittgenstein, is the vehicle for meaning and is context specific. Just as the meaningfulness of a language is governed by its grammar, so too are the activities of thinking defined by the particular frame of reference in which it is functioning. Thus, the rules for constructing meaning are products of the coherent system they regulate, rather than the starting points for the play of meaning that engenders them.[34]

31   Thiel, *Nonfoundationalism*, 10. Thiel's critique of the historical development of foundationalism is helpful and will be utilized throughout much of the following discussion. For a discussion of Dewey, Wittgenstein, and J.L. Austin from a different, Christian, perspective see Greg Bahnsen, "Pragmatism, Prejudice, and Presuppositionalism," in *Foundations of Christian Scholarship*, ed. Gary North (Vallecito, CA: Ross House Books, 1976) 241-292.

32   Charles S. Peirce, "Some Consequences of Four Incapacities [1868]," in *Collected Papers of Charles Sanders Peirce*, vol.5, ed. Charles Hartshorne and Paul Weiss (Cambridge, Mass.: Harvard University Press, 1960) 158.

33   Ludwig Wittgenstein, *Philosophical Investigations*, 3rd ed., trans. G.E.M. Anscombe (New York: Macmillan, 1968) 49.

34   Wittgenstein, *Investigations*, 138.

Building on the tradition of pragmatism, Quine and Sellars, who both reject the traditional integrity of philosophy as a special discipline for discovering truth, have worked to expose the groundlessness in Cartesian/Lockean assumptions of the theorizing in virtually all disciplines to explain their subject matter. In other words, they reject foundations of certitude, whether rationally or empirically determined, as the basis for knowledge in all types of theoretical thought. Philosophy, for Sellars, rather than being the discipline for determining objective truth, is "the reflective knowing one's way around in the scheme of things."[35]

Sellars also recognizes that it is not just the rationalists who hold to the idealist epistemology of non-inferential knowledge as first principles—empiricists do the same. The most basic of axiomatic fallacies identified by Sellars is the 'myth of the given.' This myth, he explains, is "the idea that knowledge of episodes furnishes *premises* on which empirical knowledge rests as on a foundation."[36] His targets here, of course, are the internal episodes, or principles, used as a theoretical foundation for interpretive schemes. He takes for granted that the rationalist versions of the myth are obvious as logical fallacies. But these internal episodes are not problematic, as such, but are part of the human condition. It is only when certain aspects of experience are viewed as authoritative and regarded as a foundation for other claims to knowledge within a conceptual scheme that a problem arises. John Thiel makes the comment that, according to Sellars, "this myth does not preserve a benign or higher truth but perpetuates a logical fallacy that distorts our expectations about what knowledge is and how it functions."[37]

Sellars sets the contextual parameters for the knowledge issue and the dilemma surrounding it by asking the question, "[i]f knowledge is justi-

---

35 Sellars, "Philosophy and the Scientific Image of Man," in *Science, Perception and Reality* (London: Routledge & Kegan Paul, 1963) 2.

36 Sellars, "Empiricism and the Philosophy of Mind," in *Science, Perception and Reality*, 140.

37 John Thiel, *Imagination and Authority: Theological Authorship in the Modern Tradition* (Minneapolis: Fortress Press, 1991) 174.

fied true belief, how can there be such a thing as self-evident knowledge? And if there is no such thing as self-evident knowledge, how can *any* true belief be, in the relevant sense, justified?"[38] What he is building on here, of course, is the notion that knowledge is in fact 'justified true belief.'[39] Though the definition has been debated, it seems to be the generally accepted one. By taking it as the acceptable definition, Sellars exposes the inherent problems of knowledge for the philosopher with the notion of the self-evident, or as he calls it, 'the given.'

He challenges the doctrine of 'the given' precisely on the issue of the epistemological status of foundational beliefs. In his essay, *Epistemological Principles*, Sellars critiques philosopher, Roderick Chisholm, on the points of reported knowledge and the authority of foundational beliefs. Foundational beliefs and reported knowledge, to qualify as knowledge, must, Sellars argues, be supported by an authority of some type. And the person making the report of knowledge must, in some sense, recognize the authority to be such.[40] Authority, for the empiricist, can only lie in the reliable connection between what is observed and the generalization that what has been reported by the observation is in fact true.[41] But, how is the truth of the generalization determined? To make that determination, would, of course, imply, as Sellars has noted, that there is a level of *cognition* more basic than *believing* and would consist of a sub-conceptual awareness of certain facts.[42]

38 Wilfrid Sellars, "Epistemic Principles," in *Epistemology: An Anthology*, eds. Ernest Sosa and Jaegwon Kim (Oxford: Blackwell Publishers Ltd., 2000) 125-133.

39 This explication of knowledge is, however, questionable after Edmund Gettier's strong argument rejecting it, "Is Justified True Belief Knowledge?" in *Epistemology: An Anthology*, eds. Sosa and Kim.

40 Sellars, Epistemic Principles," 125-133; cf. "Does Empirical Knowledge have a Foundation?" in *Epistemology*, 120-124.

41 Sellars, "Epistemic Principles," 131.

42 Sellars, "Epistemic Principles," 128-9; Sellars also recognizes that to speak of a "fact' assumes an entire theory of fact.

As a solution to the problem, he proposes a holistic perspective. His holistic approach to the justification of knowledge is placed in a naturalistic setting, whereby, the authority of his epistemic principles is construed in terms of "the acquisition of relevant linguistic skills."[43] While he acknowledges the authoritative nature of 'self-evident' or 'intuitive' knowledge, and that, in the final analysis, it rests on authoritative non-inferential propositions, it is, nonetheless, on his view, not to be construed as a foundation.[44]

Quine similarly holds an empirical approach to knowledge, but also rejects the notion that truth is deduced from sense data through empirical analysis. More appropriately, he argues, empirical analysis has the task of piecing together ad hoc theories derived exclusively from sensory evidence.[45] Since knowledge and philosophy's pursuit of knowledge is grounded in sense experience, there is no role for philosophy to play as an "a priori propaedeutic or groundwork for science." Philosophy provides no external vantage point from which to appropriate knowledge. But, rather, philosophy is "continuous with science" and functions as a type of empirical investigation that critically describes the process by which sensory evidence is formed into the web of concepts that make up knowledge.[46]

In his essay *"Two Dogmas of Empiricism"* Quine called into question the belief that each justifiable belief could be traced to special foundational beliefs derived directly from experience.[47] The error in this, he argues, is that the attempt to salvage a special indubitable kind of knowledge

---

43   Sellars, "Epistemic Principles," 131.

44   Sellars, "Epistemic Principles," 127, 132.

45   Roger Gibson, Jr., *The Philosophy of W.V. Quine: An Expository Essay* (Tampa: University Presses of Florida, 1982) 1.

46   W.V.O. Quine, "Natural Kinds," in *Ontological Relativity and Other Essays* (New York: Columbia University Press, 1969) 126-7.

47   W.V.O. Quine, "Two Dogmas of Empiricism," in *From a Logical Point of View* (Cambridge: Harvard University Press, 1953).

based on concepts and their relations, fails, because we are always able (and sometimes willing) to adjust the meanings of terms in order to maintain the truth of the claims. Building on this, Quinean holism requires that the whole of conceptual knowledge face the tribunal of experience, thus allowing for shifts in the meaning of concepts due to the pressure from new discoveries and theoretical changes.

Theoretical knowledge, for Quine, is context bound. That is, meaningful theories are not context-free, but are limited by their particular disciplines and unable to transcend their conceptual schemes to a universal explanation. Theories are not fully interpreted sentences and determinate explanations of their subject matter because they are always located within ever widening language contexts. Quine views this approach as holistic epistemology. The metaphor that best describes this position is a web. This web of concepts, for Quine, is a metaphor to counter the foundation metaphor. A sympathetic student and supporter of Quine, Nancey Murphy understands his holism as a belief "supported by its ties to its neighboring beliefs and, ultimately, to the whole."[48] Additionally, coherence within the web is critical for justification of belief. Justification within the web "consists in showing that problematic beliefs are closely tied to beliefs that we have no good reason to call into question."[49]

While Sellars and Quine focused on philosophical issues in general, Rorty has directed his efforts at subverting the epistemological tradition in particular. Also interested in exposing the illusion of foundations for knowledge and rationality, he takes as his investigative field the history of philosophy, unlike Sellars and Quine who address the logical framework of theories.[50] Rorty, nonetheless, acknowledges his dependence on the work of Sellars and Quine when he says,

---

48   Murphy, *Beyond Liberalism*, 94.

49   Murphy, *Beyond Liberalism*, 94.

50   John Thiel has remarked that "[a]lthough Rorty's critique of foundationalism has been one of the best known and most influential in recent years, its originality lies largely in its attention to the rhetoric of foundationalist assumptions and to the ways in which that rhetoric

I interpret Sellars's attack on 'givenness' and Quine's attack on 'necessity' as the crucial steps in undermining the possibility of a 'theory of knowledge.' The holism and pragmatism common to both philosophers, and which they share with the later Wittgenstein, are the lines of thought within analytic philosophy which I wish to extend.[51]

In his work, *Philosophy and the Mirror of Nature,* Rorty sets out to, in his words, "undermine the reader's confidence in 'the mind' as something about which one should have a 'philosophical' view, in 'knowledge' as something about which there ought to be a 'theory' and which has 'foundations,' and in 'philosophy' as it has been conceived since Kant."[52] He commences his deconstruction project by exposing the erroneous attempt by rationalist and empiricist epistemologies to privilege some aspect of mental life, or experience that grounds claims to genuine knowledge. This scheme, then, portrays thinking, or experience, as an activity with the capability to mirror reality and is the avenue for establishing a certain foundation for knowledge and belief. Rorty's argument, explains John Thiel, is that modern philosophy's ocular metaphor of the mind as a mirror reflecting the objective truths of reality encouraged the supposition that knowledge possesses a basis as immediate and as certain as a visual representation in an experience of optical perception.[53]

---

has perpetuated the foundationalist fallacy. Rorty's actual conclusions about the errors of foundationalism differ little from the principal criticisms of foundationalism that have been offered by a host of philosophers in the course of the past century. *Imagination,* 173.

51 Rorty, *Philosophy,* 10.

52 Rorty, *Philosophy,* 7, Robert Audi has remarked that "[i]t is strong foundationalism, especially the kind found in Descartes' *Meditations,* that is influentially criticized by Richard Rorty in *Philosophy and the Mirror of Nature.* Many of Rorty's criticisms do not hold for... moderate foundationalism. His doubts about the very idea that the mind is a 'mirror of nature,' however, cuts against at least the majority of plausible epistemological theories." *Epistemology: A Contemporary Introduction to the Theory of Knowledge* (London: Routledge, 1998) 209 FN14.

53 Thiel, *Imagination,* 172.

In his assessment of the history of epistemology, Rorty contends that two clearly distinguishable components to knowledge emerged. The first is the factual element given to consciousness and the second is the constructive, or interpretative, element contributed by the mind, or by language. But Rorty's contention is that Sellars' critique of the 'myth of the given' and Quine's skepticism about the language-fact distinction constitute a decisive rejection of these, mistakenly, indispensable ideas.[54] Rorty's principle argument against foundations, however, is in its use of metaphorical undercurrents for epistemic theorizing that have prejudiced the conceptualization of how knowing occurs.[55]

Equally important to the neo-Kantian epistemic project, argues Rorty, is the proposition that the aim of thought, or language, is correspondence to reality and the accuracy of representation. But in light of Wittgenstein's argument that approaches language through the notion of 'use' rather than that of 'picturing,' this proposition has also been soundly undermined.[56] The attempt to affirm the mind as the measure of certainty and to privilege philosophy as the seat of veridical authority is, according to Rorty, a misguided Cartesian desire.

Pragmatism, analytic philosophy, and the philosophy of science have successfully exposed the sorts of foundationalism espoused by the Cartesian/Lockean and neo-Kantian projects as unwitting expressions of a rationalist variety of dogmatism, which, according to many, cannot pass the test of close rational analysis. Particularly, the work of Sellars, Quine, and Rorty has been so effective and compelling that Thiel has remarked that "a consensus has been reached in the scholarly community that at least any naïve or 'strong' form of foundationalism is philosophically untenable."[57]

---

54   Michael Williams, "Richard Rorty," in *A Companion to Epistemology*, eds. Jonathan Dancy and Ernest Sosa (Oxford: Blackwell Publishers, LTD, 1992) 450.

55   Thiel, *Imagination*, 172.

56   Williams, "Richard Rorty," 450.

57   Thiel, *Imagination*, 175 It also needs to be noted here that some form of foundationalism as a theory of justification continues to be a viable epistemic position within the community of

With the ostensible collapse of foundationalism as the justificatory basis for beliefs, the obvious question then becomes—how are beliefs justified? Or, are they at all? The answer to this question is critical, not only for knowledge, but for any kind of explanation of rationality. For if what Robert Audi says is accurate, that "[b]eliefs are the basic elements of theoretical rationality," then what constitutes a justified belief is inseparable from a view of rationality. A rational belief is a justified belief.[58] And if Sellars's assumption that knowledge is 'justified true belief,' is true, then what constitutes knowledge and how it is acquired has much to do with the grounding or justification of propositions.

The main concern for this project, then, is raised again—can naturalism's foundational belief that only a material reality exists for certain be considered knowledge? According to the leading twentieth century critical thinkers above, it may be proposed, but cannot be considered a universal certainty, rather, only contextualized 'knowledge.' If this is the case, how then does naturalism qualify as the privileged view?

5.3 Knowledge and Justification

Understanding the fundamental bases for the categories religion and science has come under the scrutiny of the philosophy of religion and the philosophy of science. These relatively new disciplines exist because of the many basic questions that religion and science have not made clear. Despite the above discussion, philosophy has attempted to solve that. Philos-

---

philosophers. Several philosophers have cogently argued the case. See Roderick Chisholm, "The Myth of the Given," in *Epistemology: An Anthology*, eds. Sosa and Kim; and in *Theory of Knowledge*, 2nd ed. (Englewood Cliffs, NJ: Prentice- Hall, Inc., 1977) Hilary Putnam, "Why Reason Can't be Naturalized," in *After Philosophy: End or Transformation?* eds. Baynes, Bohman, and McCarthy (Cambridge, Mass.: MIT Press, 1987) and William Alston, "Has Foundationalism Been Refuted?" *Philosophical Studies* 29 (1976) 300-302; and "Two Types of Foundationalism," *Journal of Philosophy* 73 (1976) 171; Alvin Plantinga, *Warrant and Proper Function* (Oxford: Oxford University Press, 1993); Robert Audi, *Belief, Justification, and Knowledge* (Wadsworth Publishing Co., 1998).

58   Audi, *The Architecture of Reason*, 195-6.

opher of science, Alex Rosenberg, makes this comment about philosophy and science;

Philosophy deals with two sets of questions: First, the questions that science – physical, biological, social, behavioral cannot answer now and perhaps may never be able to answer. Second, the questions about why the sciences cannot answer the first lot of questions.[59]

How much progress is being made is questionable, however. The current transformation in the discipline of philosophy is making continued dialogue with religion and science regarding knowledge even more difficult.[60]

Some contemporary philosophers take the view that philosophy is at a turning point in need of transformation, and some are simply calling for its end as a specialized discipline questioning the value of the 'philosophy' of anything. One thing is certain, the classical philosophical categories of metaphysics, epistemology, and ethics have all come under critical scrutiny. The editors of *After Philosophy: End or Transformation?*, Kenneth Baynes, James Bohman, and Thomas McCarthy, have categorized contemporary philosophers into two groups; the end-of-philosophy thinkers and the transformation-of-philosophy thinkers.[61]

All of these philosophers, or postphilosophers as they have been termed, reject Cartesian and neo-Kantian epistemology on several counts, which include: regarding the subject of knowledge and action as punctual, atomistic, and disembodied; rational autonomy in terms of an ideal of

---

59 Alex Rosenberg, *Philosophy of Science* (London: Routledge, 2000) 4.

60 Much of the following discussion on the status of contemporary philosophy was gleaned from Baynes, Bohman, and McCarthy, "General Introduction," *After Philosophy*.

61 Representatives of the end-of-philosophy group are Rorty, Derrida, Foucault and Lyotard. The transformation-of-philosophy group is sub-divided into herneneutics, which includes Ricour and Gadamer, and systematic philosophers, which includes Putnam, Habermas, MacIntyre and Davidson.

total disengagement; appeals to immediate, intuitive self-presence as the basis of self-knowledge; and full self-transparence as a sensible ideal of self-knowledge.[62] Additionally, they have all made the 'linguistic turn,' pursuing Nietzsche's idea that philosophical texts are rhetorical constructs. While all start from the pluralism of language games and forms of life, not all agree that this is an *irreducible* pluralism of *incommensurable* language games.[63]

These disagreements are manifest in at least three areas, the first being the area of truth. The end-of-philosophy group understands truth to be totally immanent and contextually derived while the transformation group understands it to have a transcendent aspect. The second area is that of knowledge. The transformers want to continue inquiry and critical reflection, which, in their minds, will bring about greater understanding. Those who want to see an end to philosophy claim, however, that the notion that true meaning is discoverable through inquiry is a fallacy due to the essential undecidability of meaning. And the third area dividing the end/transformation of philosophical approaches is the role of theory in philosophy generally, and philosophy's relation to the human sciences particularly. The end-of-philosophy advocates oppose the continuation of theoretical philosophy while the transformation group conceives of their work to be a continuation of *practical,* and not *theoretical,* philosophy.[64]

The end-of-philosophy thinkers, who will be the main focus here, include Sellars, Quine, and Rorty.[65] Several distinctive features affecting epistemology in particular, characterize this group of philosophers. Opposition to strong conceptions of reason and the autonomous rational self, contingency, and conventionality, are fundamental to their view. The first significant implication of this position is the decenteredness of the human

---

62   "General Introduction," *After Philosophy,* 8.

63   "General Introduction," *After Philosophy,* 7.

64   "General Introduction," *After Philosophy,* 7-16.

65   The editors of *After Philosophy* do not specifically list Quine and Sellars in their groupings.

rational subject as discussed above. The rational subject for this group is decentered with the most poignant expression in the area of knowledge. Knowledge for this group is "essentially embodied and practically engaged with the world, and the products of our thought bear ineradicable traces of our purposes and projects, passions and interests...[T]he epistemological and moral subject has been definitely decentered and the conception of reason linked to it irrevocably desublimated."[66] In this view reason and knowledge have lost their transcendent nature.

Another salient implication is that the traditional notion of *knowledge as representation* has been replaced with the concept that "the object of knowledge is always already preinterpreted, situated in a scheme, part of a text, outside which there are only other texts." From this perspective, then, "the subject of knowledge belongs to the very world it wishes to interpret." The condition for forming disinterested representations of the world is engagement with it and the kinds of representations formed will depend on the kind of dealings experienced with it. Thus, underlying propositional knowledge "is a largely inarticulate and unarticulatable grasp of the world that we have as agents within it...who are essentially embodied and the locus of orientations and desires that we never fully grasp or control." The idea of a knowing subject disengaged from the body and from the world, therefore, makes no sense. For there is no knowledge without a background, and that background can never be wholly objectified.[67]

The picture revealed here clearly represents a discipline that is experiencing a radical departure from Cartesian/neo-Kantian philosophical reflection. Descartes looked for intuitive certainty in his cultural crisis while today's postphilosophers question that wisdom and find the very idea of certitude unacceptable. The shift in epistemic emphasis has not only chastened rationality, but also undermined Kant's critique of pure reason.

---

66   "General Introduction," *After Philosophy*, 4.

67   "General Introduction," *After Philosophy*, 4-5.

Rationality, then, for postmodernity seems to reside within particular contexts and is significant, pragmatically, for the purpose of finding one's way around within them. It also seems clear that modernity's claim to a privileged position for autonomous reason has come to an end. As an alternative to autonomy, Quine offers the beginnings of a more modest proposal for an appropriate contemporary description of knowledge and rationality when he writes,

> Much that we know does not count as science [knowledge], but this is often less due to its subject matter than to its arrangement. For nearly any body of knowledge that is sufficiently organized to exhibit appropriate evidential relationships among its constituent claims has at least some call to be seen as scientific. What makes for science is system, whatever the subject. And what makes for system is the judicious application of logic. Science is thus a fruit of rational investigation.[68]

If Quine's understanding can be taken as representative of the postphilosophers,[69] then rationality includes the employment of normative logic for the organization of knowledge in order to "exhibit appropriate evidential relationships among its constituent claims." Another way to express it is that rationality is conformity to the relationships of knowledge organized

---

68   Quine, *The Web*, 3.

69   Not all postphilosophers agree with Quine's view of rationality. Hilary Putnam contends that Quine's conflicting views on epistemology confuse his position on normative rationality. Quine, explains Putnam, rejects metaphysical realism and affirms bivalence (the principle that every sentence in the ideal scientific language is either true or false). Quine's position on metaphysical realism and bivalence is incoherent, argues Putnam. Quine confuses the epistemological issue with his version of a "naturalized epistemology," which attempts to reduce mentalistic notions to materialistic ones. This position, says Putnam, "is sheer epistemological eliminationism," which attempts to abandon "notions of justification, good reason, warranted assertion, and so on," in favor of the evidence of sensory stimulation. Quine's "naturalized epistemology," attempts to eliminate the normative, which, in Putnam's words is "attempted mental suicide." Putnam, "Reason," 239-242; The postphilosophers do not necessarily want to rule out the normative, but they do want to define its limitations.

by the deductive laws of logic and has an 'instrumental' function only. Not that this notion is necessarily new, but it reflects a more moderate (chastened) perspective with respect to the limitations of reason. In the following schema, Sellars addresses the function of deductive logic in producing inferential knowledge. On his account "logical implication transmits reasonableness" with the transmission via 'probabilistic' implication. He explains,

> It is reasonable, all things considered, to believe p; So, p; p probabilistically implies q to a high degree; So, all things considered, it is reasonable to believe q.

> Probabilistic justification of beliefs in accordance with this pattern would, presumably, be illustrated by inductive arguments and theoretical explanations. In each case, we move from a premise of the form:

> It is reasonable, all things considered, to believe E, where 'E' formulates the evidence, to a conclusion of the form:

> It is reasonable, all things considered, to believe H, where 'H' formulates in the first case a law-like statement and in the second case a body of theoretical assumptions.[70]

This simple formulation demonstrates the extent of the function of logic for Sellars. Quine and Sellars hold similar views on reason, at least in terms of its linear deductive function. Reason, or logic, is the method that deduces one belief from another and forms a coherent system of beliefs, which, then, constitutes rationality. But the question of justification still remains unanswered.

If there is no indubitable foundation for grounding beliefs, then what constitutes justification for the postphilosophers? The answer is that

---

70   Sellars, "Epistemic Principles," 126-7.

although many postphilosophers hold to a weak foundationalism, most hold to some type of coherentist theory of belief justification.[71] With the coherentist account, beliefs are not grounded to a base of noninferentially known certitudes. But what distinguishes a coherence theory from a foundationalist theory? Donald Davidson answers that it "is simply the claim that nothing can count as a reason for holding a belief except another belief."[72] In other words, the justification of a belief depends on its coherence with the other beliefs one already holds to be true. For the coherentist, nothing exists outside the totality of one's beliefs with which to test or compare new propositions. All that counts as evidence or justification for a proposed belief, explains Davidson, "must come from the same totality of belief to which it belongs."[73] The authority for justification resides not in the certainty of "the given," or the "self-evident," but in a network of mutually supportive beliefs.

The postmodern outlook has adopted cultural context, or conceptual scheme, as the necessary and exclusive reference point for reflection and analysis.[74] What is rejected is the Cartesian/Kantian ideal of an objective perspective outside of one's particular context as the vantage point for evaluation. No transcendent universal exists, or at least none that is accessible, by which to objectively evaluate one belief against another. As Rorty explains it, "nothing counts as justification unless by reference to what we already accept, and that there is no way to get outside our beliefs and our language so as to find some test other than coherence."[75] So, in postmodern thought, the interpreting subject is context bound, and what

---

71   For the numerous types of coherentism see Robert Audi, *Epistemology*, 178-208 and Keith Lehrer, "Coherentism," in *A Companion to Epistemology*, eds. Jonathan Dancy and Ernest Sosa (London: Blackwell Publishers, 1992) 67-70.

72   Donald Davidson, "A Coherence Theory of Truth and Knowledge," in *Epistemology*, eds. Sosa and Kim, 156.

73   Davidson, "Coherence Theory," 162.

74   See Donald Davidson, "On the Very Idea of a Conceptual Scheme," in *Inquiries into Truth and Interpretation* (Oxford: Clarendon Press, 1984).

75   Rorty, *Philosophy*, 178.

is considered reasonable depends on the orientation of the viewer or interpreter. .

Of course the immediate claim by foundationalists is that nonfoundationalism (coherentism) is an infinite regress of beliefs that ultimately ends in relativism, circular reasoning, or skepticism.[76] In the absence of foundations, they maintain that the task of justifying belief would lead to an infinite regress in the logic of justification and Locke's fear of the enthusiasts' "anything goes" attitude would certainly be a legitimate conclusion. The thought is that without a terminal point to ground beliefs, then no final authoritative claim could be reached and opinion would multiply endlessly.

This claim, though a viable one, has been addressed by the coherentists. The assumption in the claim, then, is that justification must be finite and a foundation provides the only means for insuring it. From a practical standpoint, the notion of an infinite regress is highly unlikely simply due to time and human patience. Davidson comments that, "giving reasons never comes to an end,"[77] but the regress eventually stops when sufficient warrant (whatever that might be) for the belief in question is reached. Though the possibility of an infinite set of beliefs is unlikely, having a sufficient quantity to warrant a finite regress is not. Coherentist, Michael Williams, explains that "at any given time we must have some stock of beliefs which are not thought to be open to challenge, though any one of them may come under fire."[78] But this is not unusual; it is as per design. All beliefs within a conceptual coherent scheme are susceptible to criticism. As Sellars once put it, basic beliefs are vulnerable, "though not *all* at

---

76 Robert Audi discusses four ways in which to understand the epistemic regress problem—infinite epistemic chains, circular epistemic chains, epistemic chains terminating in belief not constituting knowledge, and epistemic chains terminating in knowledge. *Epistemology*, 182-6.

77 Davidson, "Coherence Theory," 156.

78 Michael Williams, *Groundless Belief: An Essay on the Possibility of Epistemology* (New Haven, Conn.: Yale University Press, 1977) 83-4.

once...because it is a self-correcting enterprise which can put *any* claim in jeopardy."[79]

The remaining issue is the one of the incommensurability of conceptual schemes, which is inherent within postmodern coherentism. How are conceptual schemes (worldviews) to be compared and contrasted with respect to value and truth? If all worldviews are independent, self-contained systems of belief with no common ground between them, then no means exist for making value judgments between one view and another. Once reason is denied its transcendent capabilities, judgments then become intuitive, relative, and subjective assertions. Judgments regarding truth and error, good and evil, right and wrong, in any absolute sense, cannot be made. If this is the case, then what difference does it make what anyone, individually or collectively, believes?

All worldviews, then, are ultimately of equal value and equally meaningful. Philosophical naturalism, for instance, has no rational basis for making its exclusive claim to knowledge and truth, but it still makes it. From Hume, to Kant, to Nietzsche, to Freud, to Russell, to the contemporary 'new atheists,' philosophical naturalists have affirmed that only the material world is knowable. Many have additionally asserted that not only is the material world all that is knowable, it is all that exists. A non-material reality does not exist, they maintain. These are epistemological and metaphysical claims, which qualify as clear and distinct ideas positioned as foundational beliefs. A foundation is necessary for naturalism. These beliefs are the presuppositions, the first philosophy, the 'givens' for philosophical naturalism. Many agree with Carl Sagan's now famous proclamation, "the cosmos is all that is or ever was or ever shall be."[80] This is a truth claim about existence and the nature of reality—a claim to knowledge. However, no proof or evidence is offered for these most basic postulated

---

79   Sellars, "Epistemic Principles," 132.

80   Carl Sagan, *The Cosmos* (New York: Random House, 1980) 4.

beliefs. Rather, the claims are, in the words of philosopher of science, John Lennox, "not a statement of science, but of his personal belief."[81]

5.4 Summary

The purpose of the foregoing discussion was twofold; one, to reveal the general and contemporary philosophical context in which naturalism is situated, and two, to explore this context in some detail as it relates to questions of epistemology, the concept of rationality, and the religion/science dichotomy. To be sure, current philosophical debate includes more than just the topic of reason and epistemology. However, the discussion was delimited intentionally in order to highlight the fundamental philosophical elements facing naturalism and the idea of religion. It was necessary for a greater understanding of naturalism's position by exploring the philosophical developments and specific philosophers from the late nineteenth century to the present, with an emphasis on epistemology. The twentieth century philosophical ethos has left its mark not only with Kuhn and his views on paradigm shifts and normal science, but also with theism and the so-called religious views. As was noted above, the collapse of epistemological foundationalism, in the view of many, has left modernity bankrupt.

If the current state of philosophy is reasonably close to the above characterization, then any possible application of its conclusions by philosophical naturalism or theism may seem extremely remote. Justified knowledge, therefore, depends on epistemic assumptions that classical foundationalism and current nonfoundational criticism alike have rendered unwarranted. Previous chapters explored modern theism's commitment to the principles of Cartesian/Lockean epistemology and its eventual failure due to its inability to produce satisfactory evidence that met the criteria for knowledge required by classical foundationalism. As a conse-

---

81   John Lennox, *God's Undertaker: Has Science Buried God?* (Oxford: Lion Hudson plc, 2009) 30.

quence, theism was relegated to an irrelevant non-science and put out of the mainstream of intellectual dialogue. This chapter explored the impact of the postmodern project on philosophical naturalism and it, similar to theism, was found to be lacking rational justification.

Moreover, modern empirical positivism and postmodern versions of 'naturalized' epistemology find any claims to knowledge from privileged assumptions, whether empirically or rationally generated, unwarranted. That philosophical naturalism is inextricably bound to propositions that are epistemically foundational presents an obvious problem. It seems that the philosophy of naturalism as a worldview has based its concept of knowledge on a 'metaphysical' naturalism that cannot withstand current critical thought.

A critical analysis of the influences of twentieth century thought on naturalism is overdue. Philosophy has critiqued itself and found that it was lacking. As a result, postmodern philosophers, like their Cartesian predecessors, have placed a challenge before all who claim to have knowledge. But the rules that now qualify acceptable knowledge have changed and naturalists need to be aware of that. However, awareness is only part of the program of self-evaluation. Position adjustments also need to be made. How can exclusive knowledge and truth continue to be claimed by naturalists without forfeiting consistency and, therefore, integrity?

According to twentieth century critical thought, truth claims cannot be universal without a foundation of certainty, but are relative to a particular context. Truth claims only apply within a particular context, or conceptual scheme, or worldview. Different worldviews are, then, incommensurate. Within the postmodern context there is no common ground from which to judge the truth or error of the belief system as a whole. Any worldview claiming exclusive knowledge and privilege would, therefore, be misinformed and misguided. To be rationally justified, philosophical naturalism, as well as theism, need to prove their first principles—the presuppositions to their worldviews. As philosopher, David Naugle, has rightly stated, "[t]he struggle over first principles marks the human condition."[82] For theism, the existence of God must be rationally demonstrated, and for philosophical naturalism, that matter only exists and is eternal are presuppositions that must also be rationally demonstrated. If neither can do this, then skepticism or fideism (a type of skepticism) must be affirmed. Both skepticism and fideism assume that basic things are not clear to reason (not readily knowable) and each, then, fails to rationally justify knowledge, which therefore ends in meaninglessness. In other words, if one cannot determine which view is based on knowledge and which is not, how does one make a meaningful choice about anything? What criteria are used to choose one view over another? If one cannot know, then the choice is based on intuition or feelings. If one cannot know, then the choice makes no ultimate difference—it is essentially a meaningless choice.

In summation, the demise of epistemic foundationalism, of the Cartesian and Lockean variety at least, seems for many thinkers in the twentieth century to be a foregone conclusion. What were thought by Enlightenment standards to be 'givens' and foundational building blocks for knowledge no longer retain that privileged position. Self-evident truths and certainty once believed to be found in universal norms or standards, which could be determined either empirically (Locke) with uninterpreted sensations, or rationally (Descartes) with logically unchallengeable ideas, is now suspect. What has become clear to the postphilosophers is that the Enlightenment dream of a universal standard of rationality, a single method for determining truth and error and universally acceptable common ground for conversation, are Enlightenment ideals of modernity rooted in epistemic foundationalism that have been undermined by twentieth century criticism. Stout's pronouncement that the basis for a foundational type cognitive structure seems to have truly come undone, has been tak-

---

82   David K. Naugle, *Worldview: The History of a Concept* (Grand Rapids: William B. Eerdmans Publishing Co., 2002) xvii.

en seriously.[83] Foundationalism, born of enlightened critical philosophic reflection, has been determined to have missed the mark and has, indeed, been declared bankrupt.

Postphilosophers have argued that this type of knowledge theory has led to the erroneous view that beliefs are justified by an objective demonstration of proof and evidence. There is no god's eye view from which to objectively make value judgments. There is no way to objectively judge between truth and error. The current epistemic atmosphere precludes it. Proof and evidence are perspectival in nature and epistemological relativism has determined that what can be considered 'true' is true only for a specific context.

The epistemological movement in the twentieth century undermined the entire structure, foundation and all, upon which naturalism has been constructed, thus the "science wars" mentioned above. Privileged assumptions postulated as starting points for rational reflection were challenged and reduced to presumptive subjectivism by pragmatic philosophers. Cartesian axiomatic givens as certain truths, objective vantage points, knowledge as a subjugation of reality by the mind, and true statements as a direct and exhaustive mirroring of reality in propositional form are all ideals determined to be unattainable. These and many other attempts by Western philosophy to achieve indubitable knowledge about the nature of reality have all collapsed under the heavy scrutiny of contemporary intellectual thought. Achieving an objective perspective for a privileged view of reality and for grasping truth, which naturalism claims, is not to be had, according to many of the most influential voices in recent critical thought.

In the world of postmodernity, metanarratives as grand interpretive strategies with a universal rationality to appropriate them, such as Islam, Christianity, or Darwinian evolution, have not fared well, but have been replaced with contextualized stories and contextualized rationality. Conceptual schemes, framed by 'culturally derived' sociology, psychology,

---

83   Jeffrey Stout argues that Cartesian epistemic foundationalism is now an historical fact and finished as a philosophical issue, *The Flight From Authority*, Parts 1, 2.

economy, or history that have shaped and formulated traditions by which reality is defined, make up the postmodern perspective. Human reason as the primary privileged capacity once considered able to autonomously discover knowledge of reality has been chastened and a more modest view has emerged.

In light of these twentieth century conclusions, it appears that naturalism has no rational basis, or proof, for claiming exclusive knowledge. It cannot be proven that matter is eternal, the foundational belief of naturalism. If nothing is clear, skepticism and nihilism then prevail. At best, it can only claim contextual, circular, consistency. It is only one view among many, incommensurate with all others, and unable to claim truth and, therefore, privilege. Epistemological relativism, rooted in skepticism, allows all views to have their day. None can be determined to be right or wrong, true or false, good or evil.

The postmodern ethos has removed, at least theoretically, the ostensible conflict between science and religion. The popular paradigm and dichotomy collapse due to lack of evidence on each side. If there is no rational proof to favor the God hypothesis, what rational proof is there, then, to favor the matter only hypothesis? Why should one view be believed rather than the other? How, then, can naturalism justify its claim to exclusivity? The privileged view has been reduced to feelings and power. But whose feelings and whose power qualifies as the authority?

Additionally, the implications of applied postmodernity can be, arguably, culturally detrimental. As just noted above, with no rational basis for making distinctions between true and false, good and evil, and right and wrong, then choices, whether individually or culturally, lose their meaning and significance. All perspectives on reality are of equal value. If all choices are ultimately of equal value then they are equally meaningful. If all choices are equally meaningful then they are all equally meaningless. How do cultures survive when faced with a relativistic, meaningless existence—when all views are of equal value? With these statements a relativized pluralism is magnified to its logical conclusion of nihilism.

Some 'transformation of philosophy' scholars, however, have attempted to salvage the modern project due to the unacceptable implications of postmodern thought, like the ones just mentioned. They believe that a foundation for knowledge of some type is imperative for knowledge and that coherentism (non-foundationalism) is unable to avoid a skepticism that inherently leads to various forms of subjectivism, relativism and ultimate loss of meaning—nihilism. Some of these philosophers who affirm the need for a foundation for knowledge also argue that philosophical naturalism cannot defend its most basic beliefs, its first principles, and is therefore untenable. The early part of this chapter mentioned two challenges to naturalism. The first was to challenge the very idea of a foundation for knowledge, which has just been explored. The second was to defend the validity of a foundation for knowledge and to challenge the basic foundational beliefs of philosophical naturalism, which will now be considered in the next chapter.

6

Reconstructing a Foundation
for Knowledge

THE PREVIOUS CHAPTER explained the direction twentieth century critical thought has taken with the undermining of modernity's epistemic foundation and the metanarratives of religion and science. This chapter will address whether there is a rational basis for any belief system, regardless of the category. Can a foundation for the rational justification of beliefs be established from which universal claims can be made? Is this possible or not? Additionally, as discussed in the Introduction, this chapter will examine an alternative way to more accurately divide the world's belief systems that offers a more fruitful inquiry.

In spite of recent philosophical developments eschewing the Enlightenment ideals of rationality, some contemporary scholars continue to argue for their abiding value. Modernity and the Enlightenment dream are not, however, altogether dead as this chapter will attempt to show. Some are not convinced that modernity's ideals ought to be abandoned and can be reduced to the 'myth of the given.' The Enlightenment project and its values are still alive. Philosophical naturalism, as an example, has not been deterred.

This chapter will address the second challenge to the popular religion/ science paradigm. It will defend epistemic foundationalism and clarify the need for rational justification for all views claiming knowledge, whether theism or philosophical naturalism, in order to avoid skepticism, fideism, and dogmatism. Of particular focus will be naturalism's claim that theism (religion) is irrational, or non-cognitive, as expressed in the introduction, due to its failure to rationally justify its most basic belief—that God exists. We will examine that claim as well as examine whether naturalism meets its own requirement of rationality.

It will also be argued that the category and the term 'religion,' as it has been popularly understood, is no longer useful for a consistent and meaningful advancement of human knowledge and understanding. As indicated above, it will be argued that the category and term have been misappropriated by modernity in order to advance a particular epistemology and worldview—a particular philosophy of science and religion.

6.1 The Need for a Foundation

Renowned philosophers, Jurgen Habermas and John Rawls, and Christian theologian, Wolfhart Pannenberg, are foremost representatives of the social sciences and defenders of enlightened modernity who have no interest in any type of turn to pre – or postmodern agendas, but argue for modernity's enduring value in the contemporary context. Building on Hegel and Max Weber's understanding of modernity,[1] Habermas attempts to salvage and retain a commitment to the project of modernity characterizing it in language of optimism when he writes,

---

1   See Jurgen Habermas, *The Philosophical Discourse of Modernity* (Cambridge: The MIT Press, 1987) 23-44, In this work he opposes postmodernity in favor of defending the "unrealized potential of modernity" (p.1). *Habermas and the Unfinished Project of Modernity*, Passerin d'Entreves and Benhabib, eds. (Cambridge: The MIT Press, 1997) 45, In each of these works Habermas expresses his indebtedness to Hegel and Weber. Others who understand the present to be the late stage of modernity are Hans-Georg Gadamer, Paul Ricoeur, Hans Blumenberg, Charles Taylor, Hilary Putnam, and Alasdair MacIntyre, see *After Philosophy: End or Transformation?* eds. Baynes, Bohman, and McCarthy (Cambridge, Mass., 1988).

The project of modernity as it was formulated by the philosophers of the Enlightenment in the eighteenth century consists
in the relentless development of the objectivating sciences, of
the universalistic foundations of morality and law, and of autonomous art, all in accord with their own immanent logic. But at
the same time it also results in releasing the cognitive potentials
accumulated in the process from their esoteric high forms and
attempting to apply them in the sphere of praxis, that is to en-
courage the rational organization of social relations.[2]

Though the approach by Habermas to rescue the Enlightenment dream
may be noble, the attempt, according to many as indicated in the previous
chapter, is, nonetheless, misguided and unconvincing. The same is said
about Rawls and Pannenberg. Rawls, in his *A Theory of Justice*, argues for
universal principles of social justice.[3] Pannenberg, a contemporary Christian theologian with an apologetic agenda to salvage modernity, is often
placed with theologians, David Tracy and Schubert Ogden, as pointing to
universalist versions of truth and knowledge. Pannenberg's comprehensive
work on the unity of reality as historical process discoverable by reason
qualifies him for the category.[4] For Pannenberg, the criteria for universal
epistemic justification are mainly those beliefs for which good reason can
be given, which ought to lead any reasonable person to accept them. Like
the modernists who have gone before him, Pannenberg, too, is unwilling
to give up his epistemic dependence on a foundation for reason.

The quest by Habermas, Rawls, Pannenberg, and other modernists
for universal objective standards and foundational truths that any rational
person has to believe, is, as discussed, an attempt that many believe is to

---

2   Jurgen Habermas, "Modernity: An Unfinished Project," *Habermas and the Unfinished Project
     of Modernity*, Passerin d'Entreves and Benhabib, eds. (Cambridge: The MIT Press, 1997)
     45. Habermas argues that there is a universal core of moral intuition in all times and in all
     societies, see his *Autonomy and Solidarity* (London: Verso, 1992).

3   *A Theory of Justice* (Cambridge: Harvard University Press, 1971).

4   See Wolfhart Pannenberg, *Basic Questions in Theology* (Philadelphia: Fortress Press, 1971).

do something that our preeminent philosophers tell us is not rationally possible. They argue that there is no determinable universal core of moral intuition or Archimedean point for assessing the justice of social systems or historical process as proposed by these three scholars. According to the postmodern mind, if comparative judgments about rationality need to be made they need to be made only at the level of the general structures of society. But this is to assume that reason has no transcendental or onto-logical qualities, an assumption that needs more analysis, which will be assessed in the following.

It should be apparent by now in what has been discussed thus far, that the tension between modern and postmodern thought is centered on the issue of what, if anything, can be known by reason. The issue at root level is an epistemological one. Reason, it has been argued from Hume to Kant to postmoderns, is inadequate and cannot transcend sense experi-ence within a particular historical context.

But regardless of the specific answer to the knowledge issue, Reason is an integral component of the process and uniformly upheld as instru-mental for establishing coherence and meaning in some way for moder-nity's foundationalism and postmodernity's non-foundationalism. Each approach uses Reason to construct a belief system, or worldview, and therefore considers Reason necessary for consistency and meaning.

Coherentism (non-foundationalism) allows for contextual meaning and significance to be established by the inner rational consistency of all beliefs without a recognized basic foundational belief. But the question that still begs to be answered then is, as mentioned in the previous chap-ter, how can one belief system be determined to be true and another not? Is there a rational basis for choosing one over another? Is there a way to transcend a particular historical context in order to make an objective judgment? The answer for the postmodern is, of course, no. At best, the idea of truth is reduced to a relative term within a context. A starting point for achieving certainty, an objective perspective, or god's eye view, cannot be achieved.

Postmodern thought claims that first principles, or foundational beliefs, as the starting point for Reason that are certain, are not possible. Certainty, with respect to truth, knowledge, meaning, and theories of a transcendent reality, are not possible. Essentially, judgments about anything that universalize or transcend an empirically based historical context are not possible. Since reason is limited by this context, human capacity for knowledge is also limited. We cannot have knowledge of anything that is beyond empirical observation, according to the postmodern assessment.

But this position, at least in part, is unacceptable for naturalists and some non-naturalists. Naturalists want to affirm the empirical observation part, but reject the part limiting knowledge of objective truth. But in order to do this, they need a foundation of certainty upon which to build. To respond to the incommensurability issues, a foundation must first be established contrary to postmodern criticism. A foundation for rational thought allows for meaning and significance to be established by constructing less basic beliefs that are logically consistent with rationally justified foundational beliefs. If foundational beliefs that are certain can be established, it can then provide the basis for building a belief system whereby less basic beliefs would be deduced from more basic foundational beliefs. Knowledge and consistency is the goal. Any proposition not logically consistent with the most basic belief is rejected. This then is the method for making a distinction between one view and another with respect to truth, value, and meaning. This idea will be developed further in what follows.

But what are those foundational first principles—those presuppositions upon which to build? Is there any proposition, or set of propositions, that are self-evidently true that can serve as a certain foundation for a belief system? And more importantly, are they any different than the failed Cartesian intuitively self-evident version? Without a significant change, foundationalism, just as non-foundationalism, is left with the same truth v. error dilemma. Is it self-evident that God exists or that only matter exists? Without establishing a sound basis for determining first principles, the dilemma leads to skepticism or fideism as the only alternative.

With fideism, a 'belief without proof' is required since the starting point (first principles) of Reason cannot be rationally established. This 'leap of faith' consists in each case of uncritically held presuppositions as the starting point for Reason about what can be known and how. For example, theists affirm the existence of a spiritual divine creator alone as the ultimate reality and do not offer proof for that claim. Naturalists uncritically presuppose matter alone as the ultimate reality, but they also do not offer proof for their claim.

They each insist that alternative views cannot be justified and, therefore, must be false, while claiming that Reason produces this result. But postmodern criticism claims that it does not definitively produce that conclusion. Reason is only functioning pragmatically or instrumentally (practical Reason) to maneuver within a coherent circle. On what basis, then, can one view be chosen over another? Without a new solution for establishing foundational beliefs that are certain and hence a starting point for the reasoning process, then nothing has changed from Descartes.

If a foundation for knowledge is to be salvaged by the transformation philosophers, then the strong challenges noted above must be overcome beginning with the nature of Reason and its ability to produce knowledge. To reconstruct a foundation for knowledge two obstacles will need to be overcome. First, the limitations placed on Reason need to be removed. Hume's and Kant's limitations need to be demonstrated to be false. Reason then becomes the exclusive tool of inquiry and judgment, and common ground for discourse. Second, it must be demonstrated that certainty is possible. That is, a basic belief that is non-falsifiable. If the certainty of basic beliefs can be established, then less basic beliefs can be inferentially deduced. Once these objectives are accomplished, a foundation for thought that enables distinctions to be made will then establish clarity between opposing belief systems (worldviews).

6.2 The Function of Reason

Building on the tradition of Hume and Kant, postmodernity does not reject the validity of Reason, but rejects its transcendent capability and considers it inadequate to produce universal knowledge. There are no universal criteria for rationality. It cannot tell us about anything that transcends human experience, but is only for "the reflective knowing one's way around in the scheme of things," says Sellars.[5] Peirce adds that "we have no power of intuition" to give us a firm foundation from which to launch the reasoning process.[6] For the postmodern, reason serves an instrumental, practical function only.

Thus far, three mutually exclusive views have been explored, each claiming to use Reason and each claiming to be true—theism and philosophical naturalism—and a third position, postmodernity, that claims Reason has a practical function, but that it cannot be known by Reason which view, if any, is true (skepticism).

All three are contemporary and vying for the dominant authoritative voice. The first view, theism, has already been marginalized to the non-cognitive realm. The second and third views are presently sharing dominance in the Western academy; the second view in the physical and social sciences and the third view in the humanities and liberal arts.[7] Each view claims to employ Reason to some degree as its ultimate authority, as it must. Reason for each view is the governor of consistency and is inescapable for those who think. But how disagreement is to be resolved and first principles determined are questions that still need an answer.

---

5   Sellars, "Philosophy and the Scientific Image of Man," 2.

6   Pierce, "Some Consequences of Four Incapacities," 158.

7   See Keith Parsons', *The Science Wars*, particularly pages 161-170. Parsons addresses the issue regarding the epistemological objectivism and relativism that divides disciplines in the academy.

In response to the postmodern mentality of limited Reason incapable of judgment on a normative transcendent reality, Hilary Putnam makes these notable comments, "if all notions of rightness, both epistemic and (metaphysically) realist, are eliminated, then what are our statements but noise-making? The elimination of the normative is attempted mental suicide."[8] To discount Reason's capability to transcend a context is to deny meaningful statements. Again Putnam expounds;

> Why should we expand our mental energy in convincing ourselves that we aren't thinkers, that our thoughts aren't really about anything, noumenal or phenomenal, that there is no sense in which any thought is right or wrong (including the thought that no thought is right or wrong) beyond being the verdict of the moment, and so on? This is a self-refuting enterprise if there ever was one! Let us recognize that one of our fundamental self-conceptualizations, one of our fundamental 'self-descriptions,' in Rorty's phrase, is that we are thinkers, and that as thinkers we are committed to there being some kind of truth, some kind of correctness that is substantial and not merely 'disquotational.' That means that there is no eliminating the normative.[9]

How, then, is Reason established as normative? To begin, Reason is used to postulate everything that is thought. It can be used incorrectly, but not denied without using it. It is self-evident that we think. It is also self-evident that we use the laws of thought—logic, or Reason.

If Reason is denied then intelligent thought ceases. Even to say that Reason is limited is to make a judgment using Reason. Apparently, for postmoderns, Reason is capable of recognizing the idea of a transcendent reality, but not able to postulate anything meaningful about it. To consider Reason as limited may be a judgment that ought not, indeed, cannot

8   Hilary Putnam, *Why Reason Can't Be Naturalized*, p. 241, in *After Philosophy: End or Transformation?* eds. Baynes, Bohman, and McCarthy (Cambridge, Mass., 1988).

9   Putnam, *Why Reason*, 242.

be made. It may have been misassessed. Reason is the only light human beings have to dispel the darkness.

For Putnam, Reason is not only immanent, but must transcend empirical experience to the level of a transcendent universal. "If reason is both transcendent and immanent, then philosophy, as culture-bound reflection and argument about eternal questions, is both in time and in eternity."[10] Reason would then be the means to understand that which is eternal. Adding to Putnam's comments, another transformation philosopher, Surrendra Gangadean, writes clearly and makes an even stronger claim;

> Reason is transcendental. It is authoritative. It stands above all thinking and makes thinking possible. It cannot be questioned for it makes questioning possible. It is self-attesting. It testifies to itself and cannot be testified to by another. It is the highest authority in the realm of human knowledge. The deliverances of prophets, poets, philosophers, and physicists must be in accord with reason.[11]

With these statements, reason is established as common ground for all who think. To be human is to use reason. Thinkers use the laws of reason—the laws of thought.[12] To violate a law of thought, such as the law of non-contradiction, is to reduce a proposition to meaninglessness. If a proposition contains a contradiction, then it cannot be determined to be true or false—it is meaningless. The proposition must be understood before a judgment can be made. It could be said, therefore, that meaning is

---

10 Putnam, *Why Reason*, 242.

11 Gangadean, *Philosophical Foundation*, 11.

12 The laws of thought are often considered to be the laws of logic discovered by Aristotle; the law of identity, law of non-contradiction, and the law of excluded middle. Gangadean considers these laws as "reason in itself." Reason must also be understood as "in its use" and "in us." In its use it forms concepts, judgments, and arguments and is a test for meaning. It is used to interpret experience and to construct coherent worldviews. Reason in us is natural, ontological, transcendental, and fundamental. It is not conventional, but natural and universal, the same in all who think. *Philosophical Foundation*, 8-11.

more basic than truth and reason is the test for meaning.[13] A belief system must not be constructed on a contradiction nor contain contradictions in order to avoid meaninglessness.

Reason, then, as the test for meaning, must, therefore, be the ultimate authority in matters of knowledge and truth. But can reason produce the certainty required for a foundational basic belief? If so, then how? And just as important, can reason serve as the judge of truth and error over differing contexts? These are critical questions that need an answer.

So, the first task for reason then is to produce a first principle of knowledge that can be considered certain. Since all worldviews agree that reason is used and is significant, the issue of differences and where to start the reasoning process is the fundamental concern that remains to be answered. Each presupposes a different 'given,' a different intuited self-evident first principle, or set of principles, from which to begin.

Twentieth century postmoderns have argued that there is no determinable starting point for the reasoning process because there are no first principles that can be granted the status of certainty. There is no foundational certainty that establishes a beginning point from which inferences can be deduced, but only foundationless beliefs within particular historical contexts that cohere with each other and "nothing can count as a reason for holding a belief except another belief."[14] Hence Quine's web metaphor. This is the position of postmodernity. But is it tenable? The following will demonstrate significant inherent problems with the postmodern scheme and offer reasons for believing that it is not. A foundation for knowledge can be established by reason and is necessary for meaningful human experience.

---

13   Gangadean, *Philosophical Foundation*, 9.

14   Davidson, "Coherence Theory," 156.

6.3 Certainty, Presuppositions, and Knowledge

The issues between so-called religion and philosophical naturalism that have been discussed thus far, are those regarding the fundamental nature of existence and whether reason allows us to know anything about it. What follows addresses the concept of existence and our most basic belief.[15] Existence is the field for experiencing discovery and description, that is, science, the search for truth. The idea of existence is our most basic concept. All worldviews address the issue of existence. Whether it is a so-called religion or philosophical naturalism, they interpret and explain the data of experience and existence. They affirm, either explicitly or implicitly, something about the nature and meaning of existence and most basically, what ultimately exists.

Philosophical naturalism cannot escape this issue as it too addresses the nature of existence. It makes a claim regarding what ultimately exists—a claim to have knowledge. Naturalism presupposes the eternality of matter—as stated by Carl Sagan above, that all that exists now, or ever has, is the material universe, or simply, matter is eternal. What has always existed and will continue to exist is one substance—matter. Can proof or evidence be produced to support this claim? Is this a reasoned conclusion or merely an assertion? Can the first principles of opposing alternative views be rationally defeated by this assertion? If so, how would it be done? Are there any known sound arguments establishing this point? Undoubtedly not, but rather, naturalism is dogmatically asserted and the premise

---

15 Gangadean, *Philosophical Foundation*. Gangadean makes these statements about concepts and beliefs; "the most basic concept is about existence, whether something is or is not....'it is' assumes the distinction of now and not now, whether past or future. Past and future are further distinguished by always and not always....what has not always existed is not eternal; it is temporal. It asks, 'where did it come from?' Logically, the mind must stop with the eternal. It cannot ask, 'where did the eternal come from?' Ontologically, what is eternal would be the source of what is temporal. So an eternal being is logically and ontologically more basic than a temporal being. Our most basic concept of being is 'eternal' and the most basic belief is an answer to the question 'What is real or eternal?'" (40).

that only the material world exists and is eternal functions as an unproven, uncritically held presupposition.

Renowned philosopher and staunch naturalist, Victor Stenger, says as much with his comment about naturalism and its assumption that reality is composed solely of material objects; "[w]hile it cannot be denied that most physical scientists, at least, think this is the case, they cannot prove it."[16] This is a startling admission since it comes from his book in which he argues that science proves that the most basic belief of theism (that God exists) cannot be proven and, therefore, cannot claim to have knowledge.[17] But how can such a strong position be maintained if philosophical naturalism (science) cannot prove its own most basic belief? At best, naturalism would have to accept that neither view can be proven nor claim knowledge.

It is apparent that what is fundamentally at stake with the various belief systems is the issue regarding what ultimately exists. That is, the world as we experience it seems to be temporal, to change and pass away. All that exists seems to be dependent upon something else for its existence. Since something continues to exist, there must, then, be something that exists that is self-sustaining; it does not change or pass away—something that does not die, but has life in itself. There must be something that is eternal and the cause of temporal existence. Naturalism claims that that something is the material world. It claims that only matter exists and is eternal (material monism). The material world, then, if eternal, would need to be self-sustaining and self-maintaining.

However, two additional alternative views regarding existence and eternality need to be considered in addition to material monism. The first alternative view is that 'nothing' exists eternally and the second alternative is that only 'some' that exists is eternal (and some is not eternal). So this makes three options regarding existence and eternality; 1.) the view

16   Victor Stenger, *God The Failed Hypothesis: How Science Shows That God Does Not Exist* (New York: Prometheus Books, 2007) 15.

17   See Stenger's, *God The Failed Hypothesis.*

of naturalism—*all* that exists has always existed, 2.) *nothing* has always existed, and 3.) the view of theism—only *some* that exists has always existed. These options have been explained in detail by transformation philosopher, Surrendra Gangadean. In his analysis they can be abbreviated as; *all* is eternal, *none* is eternal, and only *some* is eternal (and some is not eternal).[18] Much of what follows will explore Gangadean's proposal for re-establishing a rational foundation knowledge and certainty.

All worldviews (religions and philosophical naturalism) presuppose, explicitly or implicitly, one of these most basic beliefs about what exists ultimately. To divide the world's belief systems in this way is to reveal their differences at the most basic level. The common way of dividing the world's belief systems has been to use the natural/supernatural, or even the spirit/non-spirit models—as expressed by the popular paradigm. However, when discussing existence, the eternal/temporal distinction is more basic than the natural/supernatural or spirit/non-spirit distinctions and therefore more clear. Proper critical thinking requires that presuppositions be clarified first. While these are characteristics of some belief systems, they are inadequate for accurately dividing all belief systems. Gangadean has helpful insight on this point and is worth quoting at length;

Basic beliefs are about basic things and basic beliefs are about basic concepts. We can identify basic beliefs and their different worldviews by identifying the basic concepts. The most basic concept is about existence, whether something is or is not....'It is' assumes the distinction of now and not now, whether past or future. Past and future are further distinguished by always and not always. What has always existed in the past and will

18   This framework regarding existence (the traditional square of opposition) has been developed in detail by Surrendra Gangadean in his, *Philosophical Foundation,* chapter four. It is also worth noting here that some naturalists in recent times have proposed the idea that something can come from nothing and, therefore, the option nothing is eternal is valid. This will be discussed in more detail below.

always exist in the future is eternal. What has not always existed is not eternal; it is temporal. So there are two kinds of existence, temporal and eternal. Of these two, eternal is more basic than temporal, for two reasons. Logically, the mind cannot stop with temporal. It asks, 'Where did it come from?' Logically, the mind must stop with the eternal. It cannot ask, 'Where did the eternal come from?' Ontologically, what is eternal would be the source of what is temporal. So an eternal being is logically and ontologically more basic than a temporal being. Our most basic concept of being is 'eternal' and the most basic belief is an answer to the question 'What is real or eternal?'[19]

But before it can be determined *what* is eternal it must first be determined if it is possible to *know* that something is in fact eternal. Must there be something that is eternal? Contrary to postmodern criticism, the human mind can have knowledge about what ultimately exists and certainty can be secured at the most basic, foundational, level of thought. There must, of logical necessity, be something eternal and it can be shown to be the case. The opposite, of course (and contradictory), is that nothing is eternal. But if nothing is eternal, then what exists now would have had to have come into existence from non-existence (nothingness). To affirm this presents a contradiction and cannot therefore be true.[20]

With two contradictory propositions such as 'nothing' is eternal contrasted to 'something' is eternal, the two cannot both be true and they cannot both be false. With a contradiction one proposition is true and the other, of rational necessity, is false. A rational argument is then necessary to show which is true and which is false. If it can be demonstrated that 'nothing is eternal' is logically impossible, then its opposite 'something is

---

19   Gangadean, *Philosophical Foundation*, 40

20   To affirm existence from non-existence would be the same as the proposition existence *is* non-existence, or *a* is *non-a*, a violation of the law of identity and a contradiction.

eternal' must, of necessity, be true. Gangadean sets up a logical proof as follows:

Proof that there must be something eternal—our most basic belief.

1. Contradictory statements cannot both be true and cannot both be false.
2. The contradiction of "some is eternal" is "none is eternal."
3. If "none is eternal" then:

   All is temporal.
   All had a beginning.
   All came into being.

4. If all came into being then being came into existence from non-being.
5. Being from non-being is not possible.
6. Therefore the original "none is eternal" is not possible.
7. Therefore its contradiction "some is eternal" must be true.[21]

It is clear, Gangadean argues, that "through the use of reason, something must be eternal. For a skeptic to doubt this is to give up reason. To give up reason is to give up meaning and dialogue. 'There must be something eternal' is maximally clear since the opposite is not logically possible."[22] Contrary to a major tenet of postmodernity, knowledge of something being ultimate *can* be grasped through the use of reason, as illustrated by this proof. Knowledge *is* possible. And, it is possible at the most basic level. Existence is our most basic concept. All other beliefs are less basic and derived from our most basic belief regarding existence. We do have certainty that something must be eternal, which is our most basic concept and whether consciously or unconsciously held is our most basic belief. This certainty is the beginning, the first step, of reconstructing a foundation for knowledge.

---

21 Gangadean, *Philosophical Foundation*, 43.

22 Gangadean, *Philosophical Foundation*, 44.

As an aside, if this concept is understood as fundamental to human thought, then an argument could be made that it serves as the philosophical basis for *sui generis* religion. Perhaps the notion of the *argumentum e consensus gentium*, the general consent of mankind, or the *sensus divinitatis*, a universal sense of deity in all humans, could be grounded in a deliverable of reason, that something must, of logical necessity, be eternal. From that necessity comes the idea of the 'sacred,' the 'holy,' or a transcendent reality. What appears and has been understood to be an intuitive 'religious' awareness is actually a deliverable of reason. All rational human beings, if they use their reasoning capability critically and consistently, could conclude that something must be eternal. There is a rational basis for belief in something that transcends temporal existence. Culture then is informed and shaped by what is believed to be eternal. The next question that needs to be answered is, what is it that is eternal (a less basic belief)?

With the proposition 'nothing is eternal' logically eliminated, then the two propositions, 'all that exists is eternal' and 'some that exists is eternal' (and some is not) remain. These are the only two options regarding what has always existed. One or the other of these two most basic beliefs serve as the presupposition, the starting point, and the foundational belief for all worldviews. These two propositions are also contradictory, which means one is true and one is false. This distinction needs more clarification.

With the idea that there is something eternal in place, the question as to what it is still remains. How is 'all' to be defined? The naturalist, of course, says that matter is the 'all' and it is eternal. The 'all' is a universal 'all.' An alternative to the materialist view is a type of ontological idealism, such as held by Germans, G.F.W. Hegel and Arthur Schopenhauer, or Hindu (Advaita Vedanta), and Buddhist (Mahayana Sunyata), where all reality is ultimately monistic (of one essence) and non-material. This view states that all of reality, including what is ultimate, is non-material, or spirit. So, in the 'all is eternal' category two options exist—material monism or spiritual monism.[23]

For our purposes here the attention will focus on material monism formulated as, 'all is eternal (matter)' and the opposing proposition, only 'some is eternal (some is not eternal).' That some of what exists is eternal and some is not implies that that which is eternal brought into existence (created) that which is temporal (came into existence). This is the position of theism—an eternal non-material being brought into existence all temporal being. One or the other of these two propositions regarding existence (all is eternal or some is eternal) is the most basic belief for Buddhism, Christianity, Naturalism, etc.—essentially all worldviews. This will be shown in more detail below, but first, foundational beliefs need to be examined.

6.4 Assessing Naturalism's Foundational Beliefs

As a reminder, the thesis of this project is that the category distinction between science and religion as presently conceived is a fabrication of modernity and needs to be deconstructed and reformulated. Modernity's view of science, as expressed by philosophical naturalism, has been constructed on a foundation insufficient to produce the knowledge that it claims to have. It claims to have knowledge of the ultimate nature of existence. This position of metaphysical naturalism claims to have knowledge gained by employing methodological naturalism. But this claim is based on unproven assumptions. Yet it still makes the claim to knowledge without offering rational proof for its first principles, or presuppositions—the same charge it makes against theism. When naturalism (both metaphysical and methodological) is critically examined at the most basic level it will be shown that no such claim to knowledge can be rationally justified,

---

23   Gangadean, *Philosophical Foundation*, see chapter six for a detailed explanation of spiritual monism.

thus dissolving the dichotomy. With the dichotomy dissolved, a new way is open for assessing and categorizing the world's belief systems.

When speaking of an eternal being, a being with no beginning and no end, theologians have historically used the term aseity—a being with attributes that include self-existence, self-maintenance, and independence with life in itself. Naturalists apply these same attributes to matter. Matter must minimally be self-maintaining in order to be eternal (no beginning or end). In order for naturalism to be true, it must be demonstrated that matter is self-maintaining.[24] Can matter be demonstrated to be self-maintaining? In other words, taking an example from cosmology, once the sun and other stars consume their fuel can these burned out entities reconstitute themselves? This would be necessary for a material universe to sustain itself. Physicists, however, have discovered an aspect of the second law of thermodynamics that prevents this from happening. As an example, the burning of fuel constitutes an irreversible process called *entropy*. Representing the consensus on this, renowned British physicist, Paul Davies, states the problem this way;

At the heart of thermodynamics lies the second law, which forbids heat to flow spontaneously from cold to hot bodies, while allowing it to flow from hot to cold. This law is therefore not reversible: it imprints upon the universe an arrow of time, pointing the way of unidirectional change. Scientists were quick to draw the conclusion that the universe is engaged in a one-way slide toward a state of thermodynamic equilibrium. This tendency toward uniformity, wherein temperatures even out and the universe settles into a stable state, became known as the 'heat death.' It represents a state of maximum molecular disorder, or entropy. The fact that the universe has not yet so died—that is,

---

24   Gangadean develops this argument in great detail in *Philosophical Foundation*. 50-56

it is still in a state of less-than-maximum entropy—implies that it cannot have endured for all eternity.[25]

It would seem that due to entropy, as Davies' statement indicates, the material world and, indeed, the entire cosmos, is not self-maintaining. If it is not self-maintaining, then what enables it to continue useful existence after its 'heat death'? What regenerates it? And more importantly, the more basic question, what caused it to exist in the first place? Naturalists, of course, have precluded any non-natural cause for the existence of the cosmos, and of entropy, so must produce a natural explanation for its existence. Recognizing the inherent difficulties that entropy poses, physicists have sought an alternative approach to the issues of self-maintenance and origins. Appealing to Davies again he offers this explanation;

> By weakening the link between cause and effect, quantum mechanics provides a subtle way for us to circumvent the origin-of-the-universe problem. If a way can be found to permit the universe to come into existence from nothing as the result of a quantum fluctuation, then no laws of physics would be violated. In other words, viewed through the eyes of a quantum physicist, the spontaneous appearance of a universe is not such a surprise, because physical objects are spontaneously appearing all the time—without well-defined causes—in the quantum microworld. The quantum physicist need no more appeal to a supernatural act to bring the universe into being than to explain why a radioactive nucleus decayed when it did.[26]

While Davies, as well as others, suggests that it may be possible to explain existence from nothing without violating the laws of physics, circumventing the laws of logic may be a bit more difficult. This proposition is tanta-

---

25 Paul Davies, *The Mind of God: The Scientific Basis for a Rational World* (New York: Simon & Schuster, 1992) 47.

26 Davies, *Mind of God*, 61-2.

mount to affirming existence from non-existence, being from non-being, 'a' from 'non-a,' which amounts to affirming a contradiction.[27] To affirm a contradiction is to propose that something can exist and not exist at the same time and in the same sense. The question could be asked, what then is the difference between existence and non-existence? Davies uses reason to formulate his proposition, but then denies the laws of reason rendering it a meaningless proposition. How can a meaningless proposition be understood or be determined to be true or false? A proposition containing a contradiction must be false.

He also suggests a "weakening" of the link between cause and effect and the appearance of objects "without-well-defined causes." It is not clear exactly what Davies is arguing for here. Not 'knowing' the cause is not, 'no' cause. Uncaused events are not logically possible and if a law of thought is violated then the proposition is meaningless and, therefore, false.[28] The implications of his position *are,* however, problematic for the laws of thought. For instance, Gangadean addresses this crucial issue when he says,

> If being from non-being were possibly true, then being would be no different from non-being. If being is no different from non-being then being is non-being, which is a contradiction. It violates the law of identity and the law of non-contradiction: something is both *a* and *non-a* in the same respect at the same time.[29]

Another proponent of existence from non-existence is theoretical physicist, Lawrence Krauss. In his book, *A Universe from Nothing*, Krauss argues for why it is reasonable to believe "that getting something from nothing is not a problem."[30] The essential dilemma facing Krauss, and others hold-

---

27 Gangadean, *Philosophical Foundation*, 44-47.

28 Gangadean, *Philosophical Foundation*, 44-47.

29 Gangadean, *Philosophical Foundation*, 45

30 Lawrence Krauss, *A Universe From Nothing* (New York: Free Press, 2012) xiii.

ing this view, is that he asserts that what he is proposing is true and not false, but his system denies the possibility of distinctions. If existence cannot be distinguished from non-existence, a caused event indistinguishable from an uncaused event, and something indistinguishable from nothing, then how can true be distinguished from false? Meaning disintegrates and dialogue stops. Krauss touches on this when he says,

> 'Why is there something rather than nothing?' must be understood in the context of a cosmos where the meaning of these words is not what it once was, and the very distinction between something and nothing has begun to disappear, where transitions between the two in different contexts are not only common, but required.[31]

While Krauss seems to recognize the logical difficulties with his shifting contexts, he is, nonetheless, arguing here that it is possible for nothing to produce something—for something to come into existence out of nothing without a cause—and not just an unknown cause. He is using semantics to make his argument. If "the very distinction between something and nothing has begun to disappear," then is the distinction between true and false also beginning to disappear? How can Krauss affirm his view to be true and not false? His words and distinctions are losing their meaning. Are we to maintain the distinction between true and false, but not between something and nothing?

In response to this proposition Gangadean clearly comments,

> If being could come from non-being then there would be no distinction between being and non-being ("a" could then be "non-a"). If being could come from non-being then there could be uncaused events. There would be no way to distinguish a

---

31   Krauss, *Universe*, 182-3.

caused from an uncaused event. When basic distinctions collapse, all distinctions resting on them become meaningless.[32]

Once a contradiction becomes part of a proposition all intelligent dialogue ceases. A context of meaningless distinctions without differences
quickly morphs into a context of nihilism. Reason as authoritative and a
test for meaning is denied and is contrary to a basic claim of naturalism—
that it is the most reasonable position. With reason denied, where do we
turn, how can we know? How can we think? All the data of science needs
interpretation and to refer to Putnam once again; reason is presupposed
for interpretation... ..it is a transcendent (a regulative idea that we use to
criticize the conduct of all activities and institutions).[33] Krauss' claim to
a reasonable explanation of the data becomes meaningless. How can this
position be believed and still maintain integrity? It cannot.

If naturalism is to be considered true, then it must rationally justify
its first principles. It must demonstrate that matter is all that exists and
that it is eternal. As Gangadean has cogently argued, this cannot be done.
For matter to be eternal it must be self-maintaining and the second law
of thermodynamics (entropy) demonstrates that it is not. Naturalists have
then opted for that which exists to come into existence from non-existence, which proves to be a contradiction (existence is non-existence, A is
non-A). Naturalism cannot prove its first principles, its most basic belief.
The foundational beliefs of naturalism are not possible, not logically nor
empirically. How then can naturalism claim knowledge and privilege? It
cannot. The dichotomy between philosophical naturalism and so-called
religion collapses. Categories are significant and have a place in scholarly
inquiry, but not as modernity and the current paradigm have formulated
them. The following will reconfigure the world's belief systems in a more
objective and accurate way.

---

32   Gangadean, *Philosophical Foundation*, 44.

33   Putnam, "Reason," 228.

6.5 Worldview as a Conceptual Scheme

Much of Western scholarship has subscribed to the naturalistic philosophy assuming it is objective and neutral. Many scholars in the area of religious studies approach their research from what they believe to be a neutral position not recognizing that their uncritically presupposed naturalistic first principles preclude that neutrality. Examples include the 'classical theories of religion' where scholars like Hume, Tylor, Freud, and Durkheim attempt to interpret and explain the origin of non-naturalistic belief.

Continuing the tradition, contemporary scholars such as Samuel Preus, Donald Wiebe, and Pascal Boyer, as discussed in chapter two, also approach their research using the same naturalistic methodology that assumes objectivity and neutrality as well as the common religion/science paradigm. But if naturalism has no rational justification for its position, then it becomes just another opinion and methodology from which scholarly inquiry is made. Why should it be the privileged methodology? The popular approach can no longer be supported. It is inaccurate, inadequate, and therefore unacceptable. Perhaps it is time for a paradigm shift.

It has already been introduced above that there is a better way to understand the world's diverse belief systems than to simply divide them into natural and supernatural. While the natural/supernatural divide is relevant, it leaves too much unclear. A more accurate and satisfying approach divides belief systems at a more basic level. The notion of natural or supernatural is not comprehensive enough or basic enough. There are views that do not fall into one of these categories. Our most basic concept is about existence, whether something exists or does not exist and whether it has always existed or came into existence.[34] All views have a belief about existence. This is where the division ought to begin.

The proposed alternative approach eliminates the term 'religion' as the delimiting label for a particular category of belief, and replaces it with the term, *Weltanschauung*, an all-inclusive term for the world's belief sys-

---

34   Gangadean, *Philosophical Foundation*, 40.

tems. The term *Weltanschauung* is a German word that means 'worldview' and functions as a concept that describes a perspective of the world. All humans, individually and collectively, affirm beliefs about the nature of the world and how it works. The idea of 'worldview' offers a different framework by which to categorize the world's various understandings of reality. In its most basic sense, worldview can be understood as a set of beliefs that give meaning to one's, or a culture's, experience. As soon to be discussed, it will be shown how belief systems have analyzable formal structures that allow for grouping according to fundamental beliefs. These beliefs then produce the descriptive data of phenomenology.

The idea of 'worldview' encompasses a broad range of concepts, which includes metaphysics, epistemology, and ethics.[35] It is used to express a unified comprehensive system of concepts that forms a metanarrative and attempts to present a coherent view of existence by interpreting and explaining the meaning and purpose of the world and life in its totality. As human beings, we tend to subscribe to and place ourselves into a grand, or master, narrative that forms a type of cultural and/or linguistic framework or medium that shapes the entirety of life and thought. As such, it is unavoidably a metaphysical system and is interconnected to epistemology and ethics. The term 'religion' has become confusing. It does not have characteristics that distinguish it from what it is not and therefore lacks clarity in scholarly works. For this reason the term 'religion' ought to be replaced by the term 'worldview.'

As just discussed above, worldviews can be divided into two separate and contradictory categories. These categories are determined by what is believed to be eternal—ultimate reality. If a chart is developed that shows how the world's diverse views relate based on their most basic belief of what is eternal, it would look something like the following;[36]

---

35 David Naugle, in his *Worldview: The History of a Concept* explains this point on worldview as "a semiotic system of world-interpreting stories also provides a foundation or governing platform upon or by which people think, interpret, and know." (291).

36 The concepts and divisions here were formulated by Surrendra Gangadean in his *Philosophical Foundation*.

All that exists is eternal			Some that exists is eternal (some is temporal) (implies creation)
Dualism	Spiritual Monism	Material Monism	Theism
Ancient Greece, Persia	Hinduism	Buddhism	Naturalism	Deism, Judaism, Christianity, Islam

This chart indicates the primary division of beliefs between worldviews based not on natural/supernatural, or spirit/matter, but on the basic belief about eternal existence. The mind, logically, cannot ask a more basic question than; what has always existed? Given the belief that something is eternal, all or some, less basic beliefs are then deduced regarding what it is that is eternal. Is it matter or non-matter or both that ultimately exists? Answers to these metaphysical questions regarding the nature of existence are the answers that make up worldviews. These beliefs then produce less basic beliefs and then as a system of beliefs produce particular practices (ethics).

6.6 Project Summary and Conclusion

This work has argued that the category distinction between science and religion, as the current paradigm conceives it, is a fabrication by modernity and needs to be deconstructed and reformulated. The grounds for the two categories have been examined and were found to be insufficient. Additionally, there is no rational basis for considering naturalism a privileged view. It cannot claim exclusive knowledge. As it is, the dichotomy is perpetuated and confusion implicitly reigns.

This confusion, both inside and outside of academia, abounds. In a speech a few years ago concerning terrorism and the Islamic State of Iraq and the Levant, then President of the United States, Barack Obama, made this statement, "ISIL is not 'Islamic.' No religion condones the killing of innocents, and the vast majority of ISIL's victims have been Muslim."[37] What is the point of this statement? The President seems to be making a judgment regarding what religion is and what it is not. How clear is this statement? Is the President reflecting a universally understood concept or his personal opinion regarding the idea of religion and ISIL? While he is certainly free to express his opinion, it is offered authoritatively, highly nuanced, and at the expense of clarity of thought.

This project has argued that the reason for the confusion is due to the way modernity has defined and framed the relationship between belief systems. According to what has been proposed in this project, a more accurate assessment of ISIL is that it is a worldview (or ideology) with beliefs that give meaning and significance to its experience. Like naturalism, ISIL, regardless of whether it is considered a religion or not, is interpreting and explaining the nature of the world and how it works.

Formally and functionally, naturalism and ISIL are the same. Each view, however, has a different most basic belief from which it begins its reasoning process. They each presuppose a different belief regarding what ultimately exists. Belief systems, ideologies—essentially worldviews—are competing for the hearts and minds of humanity.

Worldviews are constructed upon foundational beliefs and result in full-orbed cultural expression. Beliefs produce consequential practices. The issue of religion or non-religion does not contribute, but detracts from the fruitful understanding of cultural expression.

The confusion over how to understand the religion category is only part of the problem, however. Enlightened modernity has sought rational clarity and knowledge against the dictates of dogmatism and personal opinion. While the value of reason and empirical investigation have been highlighted as modernity's exclusive means to achieve certainty, clarity, and truth, naturalism as the method to achieve it has fallen short.

---

37 http://www.cnn.com/2014/09/10/politics/transcript-obama-syria-isis-speech/

The cause of the tension between the religion/science categories has been explored with workable definitions offered. It was argued that all belief systems formally function for the purpose of giving meaning to experience. All views then, whether considered 'religious' or not, serve the same function and purpose. This point alone should be enough to dissolve the paradigm and dichotomy. However, naturalism has resisted this thought, which necessitates a stronger argument. Historical support was needed.

The category dichotomy between science and religion developed in conjunction with the intellectual developments through the modern period with an emphasis on epistemology. As a result of the intellectual climate of the day, modern science took a particular direction. Subsequent to the cultural crisis created by the Protestant Reformation, an environment consisting of questions surrounding the nature of authority, knowledge, reason, and certainty were of central concern. Consequently, the subject of epistemology, 'is knowledge possible' was a formidable question—one to which modern philosophy attempted to respond.

The rise and development of Western modernity with its particular emphasis on the move from science within a Christian theistic framework to a non-theistic philosophy of naturalism was explored. As the new science transformed into a worldview philosophy and gained dominance, the once commanding Christian theistic view declined and was then marginalized and determined irrelevant for dialogue in the public square. Views incommensurate with the new empirical naturalism were categorized, beginning with Christianity, as religion, which would then ultimately become an expanded class and represented by the term, World Religions. These views opposing naturalism, these World Religions, needed their origins, beliefs, and practices interpreted and explained to which religion theorists responded with a new academic discipline—the science of religion. The basic question of David Hume would then need to be addressed, from whence did these belief systems—these religions—arise?

The religion/science paradigm was assessed by two contemporary challenges. Each specifically challenged naturalism's claim to exclusive knowledge, however, from different perspectives. The first challenge explained the epistemological strategy of non-foundationalism, the epistemic basis for postmodernity that has challenged the very idea of a foundation for objective knowledge that leads to certainty. The second challenge defended epistemic foundationalism, but challenged the foundational beliefs of naturalism. It was demonstrated that philosophical naturalism cannot claim knowledge of ultimate reality, but only dogmatic opinion.

This work also argued that the category and the term, 'religion,' is no longer useful for a consistent and meaningful advancement of human knowledge and understanding. It argued that the category and term have been misappropriated by modernity in order to advance a particular epistemology and worldview—a particular philosophy of science and religion.

With the dichotomy and paradigm deconstructed, the project then developed a radical proposal for better understanding diverse worldviews. An alternative conceptual scheme was offered that has the potential to avoid the difficulties and connotative baggage associated with the term 'religion' and the resultant theories about origin and nature (e.g. cultural, psychological, social, etc.). The alternative term and concept is the German word, *Weltanschauung* (worldview), which is definable, comprehensive, and distinguishable from what it is not. It was argued that the concept, *Weltanschauung*, in conjunction with basic beliefs, offers a different framework by which to categorize the world's various understandings of reality and showed how this can be done. Gangadean's rational presuppositional approach was proposed as a method and conceptual scheme that establishes the basic beliefs of particular worldviews and then deduces less basic beliefs from them. When viewed as a whole it forms a system of beliefs. In its most basic sense, 'worldview' can be understood as a set of beliefs that give meaning to one's, or a culture's, experience. It shows how belief systems have analyzable formal structures that allow for grouping according to fundamental beliefs. These beliefs then produce the descriptive data of phenomenology.

This approach calls for the presuppositions of the researcher and theorist to be identified. While an objective and fair assessment of the various worldviews is the desired goal, it must be understood that no particular approach to the interpretation and explanation of these views is neutral. A naturalistic approach is not a neutral approach. All worldviews and the worldviews of 'religious studies' students and researchers assume something about the nature of what is ultimate, how it is known, and 'the good' for human beings. The conclusions drawn from these studies reflect the perspective of the interpreter/explainer. The significant question that needs to be clarified is if the understanding has been informed by and constructed on a foundation of knowledge or on one of opinion and dogma. Knowledge of the nature of existence is of ultimate value.

Bibliography

Abraham, William. *An Introduction to the Philosophy of Religion.* Englewood Cliffs, NJ: Prentice Hall, 1985.

Alston, William P. "Two Types of Foundationalism," *Journal of Philosophy* 73 (1976).

_____ "Has Foundationalism Been Refuted?" *Philosophical Studies* 29 (1976)

Asad, Talal. *Genealogies of Religion*, Baltimore: The Johns Hopkins University Press, 1993.

_____ *Formations of the Secular.* Stanford, CA: Stanford University Press, 2003.

Audi, Robert. *The Structure of Justification.* Cambridge: Cambridge University Press,1993.

_____ *The Architecture of Reason: The Structure and Substance of Rationality.* Oxford: Oxford University Press, 2001.

_____ *Belief, Justification, and Knowledge.* Wadsworth Publishing Co., 1998.

_____ *Epistemology: A Contemporary Introduction to the Theory of Knowledge.* London: Routledge, 1998.

_____ eds. William Wainwright. *Rationality, Religious Belief & Moral Commitment.* Ithaca, London: Cornell University Press, 1986.

Ayer, Alfred J. *Language, Truth and Logic.* New York: Dover Publications, Inc. ND.

Ayer, Kneale, Paul, Pears, Strawson, Warnock, and Wolleim, eds. *The Revolution in Philosophy.* London: Macmillan & Co. Ltd., 1960.

Barbour, Ian. *Myths, Models and Paradigms: A Comparative Study in Science and Religion.* New York: Harper & Row Publishers, 1974.

_____*Religion and Science: Historical and Contemporary Issues.* San Francisco: Harper Collins Publishers, 1997.

Baynes, Kenneth, James Bohman, and Thomas McCarthy, eds., *After Philosophy: End or Transformation?* Cambridge, Mass., 1988.

Becker, Carl. *The Heavenly City of the Eighteenth-Century Philosophers.* New Haven: Yale University Press, 1932.

Bellah, Robert. *Beyond Belief: Essays on Religion in a Post-Traditional World.* NewYork: Harper and Row Publishers, 1970.

Berger, Peter. *The Heretical Imperative.* Garden City, NY: Anchor Press/ Doubleday,1980.

Berger, Peter, and Thomas Luckman. *The Sacred Canopy: Elements of a Sociological Theory of Religion.* Garden City, N.Y.: Doubleday, 1967.

Blanchard, Brand. *Reason and Belief.* London: George Allen & Unwin Ltd., 1974.

Boyer, Pascal. *Religion Explained.* New York: Basic Books, 2001.

Bozeman, Dwight. *Protestants in an Age of Science: The Baconian Ideal and Antebellum American Religious Thought.* Chapel Hill: The University of North Carolina Press, 1977.

Bratt, James D., ed. *Abraham Kuyper: A Centennial Reader.* Grand Rapids: William Eerdmans Publishing Co., 1998.

Brooke, John Hedley. *Science and Religion: Some Historical Perspectives.* Cambridge, UK: Cambridge University Press, 1991.

Buckley, Michael J. *At the Origins of Modern Atheism.* New Haven, CT: Yale University Press, 1987.

Burtt, E.A. *The Metaphysical Foundations of Modern Science.* New York: Doubleday Anchor Books, 1954.

Casanova, Jose. *Public Religions in the Modern World.* Chicago: The University of Chicago Press, 1994.

Clayton, Philip and Simpson, Zachary, eds. *The Oxford Handbook of Religion and Science.* Oxford: Oxford University Press, 2009.

Clifford, W.K. *Lectures and Essays.* London: Macmillan, 1879.

Clouser, Roy. *The Myth of Religious Neutrality*. Notre Dame: University of Notre Dame Press, 2005.

Coulson, Charles A. *Science and Christian Belief*. Chapel Hill, NC: The University of North Carolina Press, 1955.

Dancy, Jonathan, and Ernest Sosa, eds. *A Companion to Epistemology*. Oxford: Blackwell Publishers, LTD, 1992.

Davidson, Donald. *Inquiries into Truth and Interpretation*. Oxford: Clarendon Press,1984.

Davies, Paul. *The Mind of God: The Scientific Basis for a Rational World*. New York: Simon & Schuster, 1992.

Dawkins, Richard. *The God Delusion*. New York: Houghton Mifflin Co. 2006.

Dennett, Daniel. *Breaking the Spell: Religion as a Natural Phenomenon*. London: Penguin Books, LTD, 2006.

Descartes, Rene. *Discourse of Method and Meditations*. Indianapolis: The Library of Liberal Arts, ND.

Dillenberger, John. *Protestant Thought And Natural Science: A Historical Interpretation*. London: Collins Clear-type Press, 1960.

Draper, John W. *History of the Conflict between Religion and Science*. New York: D. Appleton & Co., 1874.

Dubuisson, Daniel. *The Western Construction of Religion*. Baltimore: Johns Hopkins University Press, 1993.

Durkheim, Emile. *The Elementary Forms of Religious Life*, trans. Karen Fields (NewYork: The Free Press, 1995 [1912])

Eliade, Mircea. *The Sacred and the Profane*. New York: Harcourt Brace &Co., 1959.

Evans-Pritchard, E.E. *Theories of Primitive Religion*. Oxford: Oxford University Press, 1963.

Feuerbach, Ludwig. *The Essence of Christianity*. Buffalo: Prometheus Books,1989.

Fitzgerald, Timothy. *The Ideology of Religious Studies*. New York: Oxford University Press, 2000.

Fuller, Donald, and Richard Gardiner, "Reformed Theology At Princeton And Amsterdam In The Late Nineteenth Century," *Presbyterian: Covenant Seminary Review*, (21/2, 1995).

Gangadean, Surrendra. *Philosophical Foundation: A Critical Analysis of Basic Beliefs*. Lanham: University Press of America, Inc., 2008.

Gay, Peter. *The Enlightenment: An Interpretation*. New York: Alfred A. Knopt, 1966.

_____ ed. *The Enlightenment*. New York: Simon and Schuster, 1973.

Gergen, Kenneth. *The Saturated Self: Dilemmas of Identity in Contemporary Life*. New York: Basic Books, 1991.

Gibson, Roger, Jr. *The Philosophy of W.V. Quine: An Expository Essay*. Tampa: University Presses of Florida, 1982.

Gillespie, Neal. *Charles Darwin and the Problem of Creation*. Chicago: University of Chicago Press, 1979.

Graham, Gordon. *The Shape of the Past: A Philosophical Approach to History*. Oxford: Oxford University Press, 1997.

Grenz, Stanley. *Beyond Foundationalism: Shaping Theology in a Postmodern Context*. Louisville: Westminster John Knox Press, 2001.

Grenz, Stanley, and Roger Olson. *Twentieth Century Theology*. Downers Grove: Intervarsity Press, 1997.

Habermas, Jurgen. *The Philosophical Discourse of Modernity*. Cambridge: The MIT Press,1987.

Harris, Sam. *The End of Faith*. New York: W.W. Norton & Co., 2005.

Harrison, Peter. *'Religion' and the Religions in the English Enlightenment*. New York: Cambridge University Press, 1990.

Hart, Trevor. *Faith Thinking: The Dynamics of Christian Theology*. Downers Grove: InterVarsity Press, 1995.

Hart, D.G., ed. *Reckoning With the Past: Historical Essays on American Evangelicalism from the Institute for the Study of American Evangelicals*. Grand Rapids: Baker Books, 1995.

Hartshorne, Charles, and Paul Weiss, eds., *Collected Papers of Charles Sanders Peirce*, vol. 5. Cambridge, Mass.: Harvard University Press, 1960.

Harvey, David. *The Condition of Postmodernity*. Oxford: Basil Blackwell, 1989.

Hawking, Stephen and Leonard Mlodinow. *The Grand Design*. New York: Bantam Books, 2010.

Helseth, Paul, "B. B. Warfield's Apologetical Appeal To 'Right Reason': Evidence of a Rather Bald Rationalism?" *Scottish Bulletin of Evangelical Theology, 16.2* (Autumn 1998)

Hick, John. *An Interpretation of Religion: Human Responses to the Transcendent*. New Haven: Yale University Press, 2005.

Hodge, Charles. *Systematic Theology, Vol. II*. Grand Rapids: Eerdmans Publishing Co., [1873] 1968.

_____What is Darwinism? And Other Writings on Science and Religion. Grand Rapids: Baker Books, [1874] 1994.

Hoeveler, David. *James McCosh And The Scottish Intellectual Tradition*. Princeton, NJ: Princeton University Press, 1981.

Hume, David. "An Enquiry Concerning the Human Understanding," in *Dialogues and Natural History of Religion*, ed. J.C.A. Gaskin. Oxford: Oxford University Press, [1748] 1993.

Huxley, Thomas H. "Science and Culture", *The Norton Anthology of English Literature*. New York: W. W. Norton & Co., 1968.

Jenkins, Philip. *The Next Christendom: The Coming of Global Christianity*. New York: Oxford University Press, 2002.

Kant, Immanuel. *Prolegomena to Any Future Metaphysics.* New York: Bobbs-Merrill Co., [1783] 1950.

_____*Reason Within the Limits of Reason Alone.* New York: Harper Row Publishers, [1793] 1960

Kaufman, Gordon. *The Theological Imagination: Constructing the Concept of God.* Philadelphia: The Westminster Press, 1981.

Krauss, Lawrence. *A Universe From Nothing.* New York: Free Press, 2012.

Kuhn, Thomas S. *The Structure of Scientific Revolutions.* Second ed. Chicago: The University of Chicago Press, 1970.

Kurtz, Paul, ed. *Science and Religion: Are They Compatible?* New York: Prometheus Books, 2003

Kuyper, Abraham. *Calvinism: Six Stone-lectures.* Amsterdam-Pretoria: Hoveker & Wormser LTD., N.D.

_____*Principles of Sacred Theology,* Trans. J. Hendrik Vries. Grand Rapids: Baker Book House, [1898] 1980.

Lennox, John. *God's Undertaker: Has Science Buried God?* Oxford: Lion Hudson plc, 2009.

Levy, Oscar, ed. *The Complete Works of Friedrich Nietzsche,* Vol. 9, *The Joyful Wisdom.* Edinburgh: T.N. Foulis, 1911.

Lindberg, David C., and Ronald L. Numbers, eds. *God and Nature: Historical Essays on the Encounter Between Christianity and Science.*

Berkeley and Los Angeles, CA: University of California Press, 1986.

Livingstone, David N. *Darwin's Forgotten Defenders*. Grand Rapids: Wm B. Eerdmans Publishing Co., 1987.

Locke, John. *An Essay Concerning Human Understanding*. Chatham, GB: Wordsworth Editions LTD, 1996.

Lyotard, Jean-Francois. *The Postmodern Condition: A Report on Knowledge*, trans. G. Bennington and B. Massumi. Minneapolis: University of Minnesota Press, 1984.

Machen, J. Gresham. *Christianity and Liberalism*. Grand Rapids: Wm. Eerdmans Publishing Co., 1923.

MacIntyre, Alasdair. *Three Rival Versions of Moral Enquiry: Encyclopaedia, Genealogy, and Tradition*, Gifford Lectures. London: Gerald Duckworth, 1990.

_____ *Whose Justice? Which Rationality*. Notre Dame: University of Notre Dame Press, 1988.

Macquarrie, John. *Twentieth Century Religious Thought*. New York: Harper & Row Publishers, 1963.

Marsden, George. *Understanding Fundamentalism and Evangelicalism*. Grand Rapids: Eerdmans Publishing Co. 1991.

_____ *The Soul of the American University*. New York: Oxford University Press, 1994.

Marsden, George, and Bradley Longfield, eds. *The Secularization of the Academy*. New York: Oxford University Press, 1992.

Marty, Martin. *The Modern Schism: Three Paths to the Secular*. New York: Harper & Row, 1969.

Masuzawa, Tomoko. *The Invention of World Religions*. The University of Chicago Press: Chicago, 2005.

McCutcheon, Russell. *Manufacturing Religion*. New York: Oxford University Press, 1997.

Middleton, J. Richard, and Brian J. Walsh. *Truth Is Stranger Than It Used to Be: Biblical Faith in a Postmodern Age*. Downers Grove, Ill.: InterVarsity Press, 1995.

Mitchell, Basil. *The Justification of Religious Belief*. New York: Oxford University Press, 1981.

Muller, Richard. *Post-Reformation Reformed Dogmatics, vol. 1*. Grand Rapids: Baker Book House, 1987.

Murphy, Nancey. *Anglo-American Postmodernity: Philosophical Perspectives on Science, Religion, and Ethics*. Boulder, Co.: Westview Press, 1997.

_____ *Beyond Liberalism and Fundamentalism: How Modern and Postmodern Philosophy Set the Theological Agenda*. Valley Forge, Penn.: Trinity Press International, 1996.

Nash, Ronald. *The Word of God and the Mind of Man: The Crisis of Revealed Truth in Contemporary Theology.* Phillipsburg, NJ: P&R Publishing, 1982.

Naugle, David. *Worldview: The History of a Concept.* Grand Rapids: W.B. Eerdmans Publishing Co., 2002.

Otto, Rudolf. *The Idea of the Holy.* New York: Oxford University Press, 1958.

Pals, Daniel. *Seven Theories of Religion.* New York: Oxford University Press, 1996.

Pannenberg, Wolfhart. *Theology and the Philosophy of Science.* London: Darton, Longman & Todd Ltd., 1976.

_____ *Basic Questions in Theology.* Philadelphia: Fortress Press, 1971

Parsons, Keith. ed., *The Science Wars.* New York: Prometheus Books, 2003.

Passerin d'Entreves and Benhabib, eds. *Habermas and the Unfinished Project of Modernity.* Cambridge: The MIT Press, 1997.

Pearcey, Nancy R., and Charles B. Thaxton. *The Soul of Science: Christian Faith and Natural Philosophy.* Wheaton: Crossway Books, 1994.

Phillips, D.Z. *Faith After Foundationalism.* New York: Routledge, 1988.

Placher, William. *Unapologetic Theology.* Louisville: Westminster/John Knox Press, 1989.

_____ *The Domestication of Transcendence*. Louisville: Westminster/ John Knox Press, 1996.

Plantinga, Alvin. *Warrant and Proper Function*. Oxford: Oxford University Press,1993.

_____ *Warranted Christian Belief*. Oxford: Oxford University Press, 2000.

_____ *Where the Conflict Really Lies*. Oxford: Oxford University Press, 2011.

_____ Nicholas Wolterstorff, eds. *Faith and Rationality: Reason and Belief in God*. Notre Dame: University of Notre Dame Press, 1983.

Preus, J. Samuel. *Explaining Religion: Criticism and Theory from Bodin to Freud* (Atlanta: Scholars Press, 1996).

Quine, W.V.O. *Ontological Relativity and Other Essays*. New York: Columbia University Press, 1969.

_____ *From a Logical Point of View*. Cambridge: Harvard University Press, 1953.

Quine, W.V.O., and J.S. Ullian. *The Web of Belief*. New York: Random House, 1970.

Reventlow, Henning Graf. *The Authority of the Bible and the Rise of the Modern World*. Philadelphia: Fortress Press, 1985.

Rorty, Richard. *Philosophy and the Mirror of Nature*. Princeton NJ: Princeton University Press, 1979.

Rosenberg, Alex. *Philosophy of Science* (London: Routledge, 2000).

Ruse, Michael. *Mysteries of Mysteries: Is Evolution a Social Construction?* Cambridge: Harvard University Press, 1999.

Russell, Bertrand. *Why I Am Not A Christian*. New York: Simon & Schuster, 1957.

_____ *The Problems of Philosophy*. London: Oxford University Press, 1959.

Ryle, Gilbert, ed. *The Revolution in Philosophy*. New York: Macmillan, 1960.

Sagan, Carl. *The Cosmos*. New York: Random House, 1980 4.

Schleiermacher, Friedrich. *The Christian Faith, Vol. 1*. New York: Harper & Row Publishers, 1963.

_____ *On the "Glaubenslehre"; Two Letters to Dr. Lucke*, trans. J. Duke and F. Fiorenza. Chico, CA: Scholars Press 1981.

_____ *Brief Outline Of Theology As A Field Of Study*, trans. Terrence N. Tice. Lewiston, New York: The Edwin Press, 1988.

Schrift, Alan D. *Nietzsche's French Legacy: A Genealogy of Poststructuralism*. New York: Routledge, 1995

Sellars, Wilfred. *Science, Perception and Reality*. London: Routledge & Kegan Paul,1963.

Sennett, James F., ed. *The Analytic Theist: An Alvin Plantinga Reader*. Grand Rapids: Eerdmans Publishing Co., 1998.

Smart, Ninian. *Worldviews: Crosscultural Explorations of Human Beliefs.* New Jersey: Prentiss Hall, Inc., 1995.

Smith, James Ward, A. Leland Jamison, eds. *The Shaping of American Religion.* Princeton, NJ: Princeton University Press, 1961.

Smith, Jonathan Z. *Imagining Religion: From Babylon to Jonestown.* Chicago: University of Chicago Press, 1982.

Smith, Wilfred C. *The Meaning and End of Religion.* New York: New American Library, A Mentor Book, 1962.

Sosa, Ernest, and Jaegwon Kim, eds. *Epistemology: An Anthology.* Oxford: Blackwell Publishers Ltd., 2000.

Stark, Rodney and Roger Finke. *The Churching of America, 1776-2005: Winners and Losers in Our Religious Economy.* New Brunswick, NJ: Rutgers University Press, 2005.

Stenger, Victor. *The New Atheism: Taking a Stand for Science and Reason.* New York: Prometheus Books, 2009.

_____ *God The Failed Hypothesis: How Science Shows That God Does Not Exist.* New York: Prometheus Books, 2007.

Strenski, Ivan. *Thinking About Religion: An Historical Introduction to Theories of Religion.* Oxford: Blackwell Publishing, 2006.

Stout, Jeffrey. *The Flight From Authority.* Notre Dame: Notre Dame Press, 1981.

Taylor, Charles. *A Secular Age*. Cambridge: Harvard University Press, 2007.

Taylor, Mark C. *Erring: A Postmodern A/Theology*. Chicago: The University of Chicago Press, 1984.

Thiel, John. *Imagination and Authority: Theological Authorship in the Modern Tradition*. Minneapolis: Augsburg Fortress, 1991.

_____ *Nonfoundationalism*. Minneapolis: Augsburg Fortress Publishers, 1994.

Thiemann, Ronald. *Constructing a Public Theology*. Louisville: Westminster/John Knox Press, 1991.

_____ *Revelation and Theology, The Gospel as Narrated Promise*. Notre Dame: University of Notre Dame Press, 1985.

Thrower, James. *Western Atheism: A Short History*. Amherst, NY: Prometheus Books, 2000.

Toulmin, Stephen. *Cosmopolis: The Hidden Agenda of Modernity*. New York: The Free Press, 1990.

Tweed, Thomas. *Crossing and Dwelling: A Theory of Religion*. Cambridge MA: Harvard University Press, 2006.

Tylor, E. B. *Anthropology. An Introduction to the Study of Man and Civilization*. Vol. 1, 2. London: Watts & Co. 1946.

Vasquez, Manuel. *More Than Belief: A Materialist Theory of Religion*. New York: Oxford University Press, 2011.

Warfield, Benjamin B. *Studies in Theology*. NY: Oxford University Press, 1932.

_____ *The Inspiration and Authority of the Bible*. Philadelphia: Presbyterian and Reformed Publishing Co., 1970.

Watts, Fraser and Kevin Dutton, eds. *Why the Science and Religion Dialogue Matters*. Philadelphia, PA: Templeton Foundation Press, 2006.

Weber, Max. *The Sociology of religion*, trans. Ephraim Fischoff. Boston: Beacon Press, [1922] 1964.

Weizsacker, C.F. von. *The Relevance of Science*. London: Collins, 1964.

Welch, Claude. *Protestant Thought in the Nineteenth Century, Vol.2*. New Haven: Yale University Press, 1985.

White, Andrew D. *History of the Warfare of Science with Theology in Christendom*. Albany, OR: Ages Software, [1896] 1997.

Wiebe, Donald. *The Politics of Religious Studies*. New York: Palgrave, 1999.

Williams, Michael. *Groundless Belief: An Essay on the Possibility of Epistemology*. New Haven, Conn.: Yale University Press, 1977.

Wittgenstein, Ludwig. *Philosophical Investigations*, 3rd ed., trans. G.E.M. Anscombe. New York: Macmillan, 1968.

Wolterstorff, Nicholas. *Reason Within the Bounds of Religion*. Grand Rapids: William B. Eerdmans Publishing Co., 1984.

_____ *John Locke and the Ethics of Belief.* Cambridge: Cambridge University Press, 1996.

_____ *Thomas Reid And The Story Of Epistemology.* Cambridge: Cambridge University Press, 2001.

Index

CPSIA information can be obtained
at www.ICGtesting.com
Printed in the USA
LVHW030201140120
643548LV00005B/464/P